PUFFIN BOOKS

Warpath 5
Last Convoy

Suddenly, there w[...]
the foredeck. The s[...]
a mass of water c[...] e
deck. Above all the noise I [...] e
howl of a dive-bomber's engine. It seemed to
be getting louder and louder.

'Look out!' shouted someone.

I spun round and saw the Stuka bearing
down on us. The starboard Oerlikons, the
Brownings and the Bofors had engaged the
plane but it continued towards us,
regardless of the fire coming at it. It was a
battle of wills: he wasn't giving up, and
neither were we. The aircraft was now
dangerously close but still it came down
without a hint that it would pull out of its
dive.

'Get down!' shouted Bill. 'He's going to
crash aboard!'

Read and collect the other books in the Warpath *series*

WARPATH 5
Last Convoy

R. ELDWORTH

A fictional story
based on real-life events

PUFFIN BOOKS

PUFFIN BOOKS

Published by the Penguin Group
Penguin Books Ltd, 27 Wrights Lane, London W8 5TZ, England
Penguin Putnam Inc., 375 Hudson Street, New York, New York 10014, USA
Penguin Books Australia Ltd, Ringwood, Victoria, Australia
Penguin Books Canada Ltd, 10 Alcorn Avenue, Toronto, Ontario, Canada M4V 3B2
Penguin Books (NZ) Ltd, Private Bag 102902, NSMC, Auckland, New Zealand

On the World Wide Web at: www.penguin.com

Penguin Books Ltd, Registered Offices: Harmondsworth, Middlesex, England

First published 2000
1 3 5 7 9 10 8 6 4 2

Text copyright © Bryan Perrett, 2000
Photographs copyright © the Imperial War Museum

The moral right of the author has been asserted

Set in 11½/15pt Bookman Old Style

Made and printed in England by Clays Ltd, St Ives plc

British Library Cataloguing in Publication Data
A CIP catalogue record for this book is available from the British Library

ISBN 0-141-30720-X

R. Eldworth is a writer's name for Bryan Perrett. Bryan is a military historian who has
written many books. This is his first title for Puffin.

Contents

Malta in Peril

In July 1942 the Allied forces in North Africa were on the verge of defeat. Throughout the desert war, the Mediterranean island of Malta had been a thorn in the side of the German and Italian commanders. At one point, the Allies were inflicting such heavy losses that only one cargo ship in five of those dispatched from Italy was reaching North Africa. The Axis were determined to destroy the threat posed by Malta, and the island had been under continuous air attack since June 1940. The garrison and the Maltese people, however, had put up a stubborn defence and the island continued to trouble the enemy.

Early in 1942 the Axis had decided to destroy the Allied resistance with a major offensive. Malta became the most heavily bombed place on earth. Allied convoys that tried to reach the island sustained such heavy losses that they were suspended. By July 1942 Malta's supplies were almost exhausted, the people near to starvation and surrender seemed inevitable.

In North Africa during the same month, the Allies had suffered one of their worst defeats. For the Axis to press on with their offensive, they were dependent upon fuel supplies, which would be guaranteed if Malta was unable to strike at the Axis supply lines. The outlook for the Allies in the Mediterranean had never been worse.

Everything depended on Malta being resupplied. The Allies decided to send a heavily escorted convoy of merchant vessels to Malta, code-named Pedestal. Terrible losses were expected, but as long as some ships got through, Malta had a fighting chance. If none got through, Malta would surrender and the success of the Allied campaign in North Africa would remain in serious doubt. It was clear the Axis would do everything in their power to destroy the entire convoy. Pedestal, therefore, became one of the most desperately fought battles of the entire war.

Our story starts in August 1942 and involves the most important ship in the convoy, the tanker *Ohio*. A young gunner of the Royal Artillery's Maritime Regiment finds himself serving aboard her and sailing straight into danger.

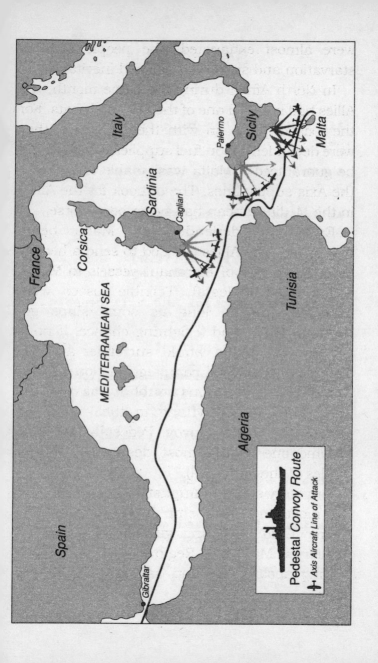

Sea Talk

Aft - towards the back or 'stern' of a ship

Abeam - parallel to the direction a ship is sailing

Amidships - in the central part of the ship

Astral navigation - fixing a ship's position by taking bearings on stars

Bilge - the part of the hull beneath the lowest deck

Bow - the front part of a ship

Bridge - the structure from which a ship is commanded, incorporating the wheelhouse and chartroom

Bulkhead - an internal partition or wall inside a ship

Cable - a strong, heavy rope OR 200 yards (one tenth of a nautical mile)

Coaming - the raised edge around a ship's doors and hatches that keeps water out

Companionway - the covered area protecting the stairs that lead down to the lower decks

Dead reckoning - tracking a ship's progress on a chart by marking its course and estimated distance travelled

Fathom - a nautical measurement meaning six feet

Hold - the space for cargo

Helmsman - the man who steers a ship

Hull - the frame or body of a ship

Knot - a measurement of speed - one nautical mile (1.14 land miles) per hour

Manilla - thick rope, usually made from a plant material called hemp

Poop - a short raised deck at the back of a ship; in tankers this was surmounted by a superstructure

Port - the left-hand side of a ship when you are facing the front

Starboard - the right-hand side of a ship when you are facing the front

Stern - the back end of a ship

This is a true story. I'd been on convoy duty before, but nothing could have prepared me for what happened on board the *Ohio*.

John Smith, DEMS gunner,
Royal Artillery Maritime Regiment
August 1942

Chapter 1
Survivor

The big four-engined Focke-Wulf Condor came in low at over 200 mph. This one had been circling our convoy for an hour or two and had suddenly dropped below the horizon. He planned to surprise us, but by now our escort vessels were used to such tricks and put up a barrage of anti-aircraft fire that forced him to take evasive action. As he roared along the centre column of ships, machine-gun fire from his lower turret shattered our wheelhouse glass and rattled off the plating. We thought his bombs had missed. But suddenly . . .

Kaboooom!

Either side of us there were two thunderous explosions under the water. The ship shook from bow to stern, and those of us on deck were drenched as water cascaded down on us. I doubted whether the plating on our old ship could withstand the shock.

We were 200 miles from safety, off the north-west coast of Ireland. Our ship, the *Mary Cranfield*, was on convoy duty. Most of my shipmates were merchant seamen but I was an artilleryman, John Smith of the Royal Artillery's Maritime Regiment. I was twenty years old and I came from Liverpool. I had joined the Army as soon as I was old enough and my rank was Gunner.

There were a few of us gunners aboard, but serving on my gun were Bombardier Bill Ryan, our detachment commander, and Ron Hood. Bill was a few years older than me, a short stocky man with years of experience etched into his face. He trained us daily and brought us up to a high standard. Ron Hood was the same age as me and had joined up at the same time. He was a tall, dark, handsome chap who always seemed to be cheerful. Officially, we were known as DEMS Gunners, the letters standing for Defensively Armed Merchant Ships.

The immediate threat of attack over, I looked around the deck for casualties and damage. Everything seemed intact, apart from the wheelhouse, but I noticed the steady thump-thump-thump of the *Mary Cranfield*'s engines had changed to a jarring rhythm of uneven and clanking sounds. Our skipper, Captain Benskin, pulled the ship out of line and the engines were stopped.

As the chief engineer hurried up the bridge ladder, the rest of the convoy passed us by without pausing. One of the destroyer escorts came up alongside.

'What's wrong?' her captain hailed.

'Bomb blast – the propeller shaft is distorted,' shouted Benskin. 'If we carry on at normal speed we'll tear the bottom out of her. Also looks like the plating of number four hold is ruptured and she's making water fast.'

'Can you make it to port?'

'We'll do what we can. The chief thinks we might get a knot or two out of her. Depends on whether we can keep the water down,' answered Benskin.

'Understood. What's your cargo?'

'General – foodstuffs mostly.'

'Right – head for Lough Foyle if you can. We'll try and get a tug out to you.'

The destroyer surged off after the convoy.

As we lay drifting in the water, I heard the sound of banging and hammering as the chief worked on the damaged prop shaft and the seamen shored up the bulkheads around the flooded number four hold. No one said as much, but we all wondered whether the Condor had reported our position to one of his U-boat pals. It must have been on the skipper's mind, too, because he gave orders for us to prepare to abandon ship. We pulled on our life-jackets and the lifeboats were swung out. Bill, Ron and I had just gathered on deck when Bill shouted: 'U-Boat!'

He pointed to port, where a black snout had begun to appear from a patch of disturbed water some 250 yards away. Behind the snout the conning-tower broke the surface. The U-boat commander obviously thought we were not worth a torpedo and had decided to sink us with his gun. Bill, Ron and I did not wait for orders from the bridge – there would have been no point. We ran to our '5-incher' as the rest of the crew prepared for the attack.

'Stand to – gun action! Semi-armour piercing – load!' shouted Bill.

We had practised the drill so many times before that it had become automatic. The 5-inch was swung to port and Bill took his place on the layer's seat. The U-boat was fully surfaced now and was running parallel to us. I shoved a shell into the breech and Ron slammed it shut.

'Loaded!' I shouted.

The gun banged immediately. I saw a fountain of spray kick up short of the submarine. Along its deck I could see tiny figures running towards their own gun. The U-boat was a Type VII, ugly and very dangerous.

'Loaded!'

Boooom!

Bill applied a correction to his aim. There was another fountain of spray beyond the U-boat. The next round should be on target.

'Loaded!'

Boooom!

There was a flash as the shell penetrated the base of the enemy's conning-tower, then exploded inside. We cheered, but in the same instant the German gun fired back. The ship shuddered.

'We're hit!' shouted Bill. 'Down low on the port side.'

There was a flickering of light on the conning-tower as a machine-gun opened up. I saw Jack Wilson and Ted Norman, two of the other gunners, fall, hit in the legs.

'Loaded!'

Boooom!

This time we thought we had hit her in the hull, but it was difficult to tell. She pumped another shell into us, then the enemy gunners ran for their hatches and the U-boat began to dive.

'We've licked 'em!' shouted Ron, and we cheered again.

'Didn't expect us to get the first one off, did they?' said Bill, well pleased with his efforts. 'They weren't bad, either – just need a few more lessons before they take us on again!'

We may have inflicted mortal wounds on the U-boat, but seconds later we realized why she had dived so quickly. A four-engined Sunderland flying boat came roaring in from the direction of northern Ireland – one of our boys. He depth-charged the area just ahead of where the enemy had disappeared, the underwater explosions sending up huge spouts of water. We could see large quantities of fuel oil and other wreckage bubbling to the surface, so it seemed that between us we'd put paid to the sub. The Sunderland then circled to see if we needed assistance. We did.

The two hits had blown further holes in

the hull on the water-line. It quickly became apparent that the pumps could no longer cope, as the ship's list grew heavier. There was a deafening hiss of escaping steam as the chief blew off the boilers to prevent further explosions. Then came the order to abandon ship. We had literally minutes before she'd go down.

I saw the skipper fling his confidential books over the side in their weighted bag. Our wounded were lifted from below into the lifeboats. The boat I was in was commanded by the second mate and, apart from Bill, Ron and myself, contained a dozen men. Most were British, but there was also a Chinese cook, a couple of Indians from the engine room, a Spaniard and an American. We pulled away to watch the *Mary Cranfield* die from a safe distance. She rolled on to her port side and slid under very quietly, stern first. No one spoke for a while.

Eventually an elderly seaman broke the silence.

'She wasn't a bad 'un when you got used to her,' he said quietly. 'Eighteen years I was aboard, and everything I own has gone down with her.'

'Same here,' replied his companion. 'All

I've got now is what I'm wearing – not much to show for a life at sea, is it?'

We watched the bubbles, coal dust and debris float to the surface. 'Aye, she was no oil painting,' said the second mate. 'We'll miss her, just the same.'

I felt sorry for these man who had lost everything. But we'd all lose even more if we weren't picked up soon.

Chapter 2
Adrift

The *Mary Cranfield* was little more than an old rust-bucket, but she had been home to all of us for a long time; in fact, we DEMS gunners had joined her shortly after Dunkirk. Most merchant ships now carried a 5-inch gun as a defence against the enemy and, as merchant seamen were classed as non-combatants, the gun had to be manned by members of the armed forces. I'd joined the Royal Artillery but had ended up as part of the Maritime Regiment.

I felt particularly sorry for the merchant seamen. Life for them was hard enough at the best of times, but their pay ceased from the day their ship was lost. Captain Benskin was a good seaman. He had the lifeboats tied together, then the sails were hoisted and a course set for the Irish coast. The

15

Sunderland hung around for a while, then made a low pass over us, its pilot waving and giving us the thumbs up to say he'd made arrangements for us to be picked up.

I had always known that this sort of thing might happen to me one day, but it was a shock when it did. In the past two years I had seen good ships sent to the bottom by torpedoes or bombs, and ships ablaze or so badly damaged that I knew they would never make port again. We had picked up our share of survivors, sometimes injured, burned or smothered in fuel oil, sometimes suffering from exposure after days in their lifeboats. They were not a pretty sight. We looked after them as best we could, knowing that next time it might be our turn.

One incident in particular came vividly to my mind. Our convoy was in the wastes of the South Atlantic, the policy being to stay out of the usual shipping-lanes in the hope that we would avoid the U-boats. A lifeboat under sail approached on an opposite course and we prepared to receive survivors. The boat came straight down the lanes, passing close to the *Mary Cranfield*'s starboard side. It was very crowded and those aboard were sitting upright; there was an officer at the tiller. Only one look was needed to see that they had all died many days earlier. Just then, the wind shifted, the officer's body moved slightly against the tiller and the lifeboat headed away, finally vanishing into the distance on its endless voyage to nowhere. I could see the more religious seamen crossing themselves. It was an eerie experience that still sends shivers down my spine whenever I think of it. For the moment, however, we were alive and a good deal nearer home.

The skipper was determined to keep everyone's spirits up. He made us sing, songs like 'Deep in the Heart of Texas', 'Show Me the Way to Go Home' and 'I've Got Sixpence' that everyone knew. We sang them so often I never want to hear them again! In between, he organized a quiz between the lifeboats, making us clap the answers to keep our circulation going, especially after sunset, when the temperature dropped.

Eighteen hours after the *Mary Cranfield* had gone down we were picked up by a Royal Naval escort sloop and taken into Londonderry. The injured men – and some of the older hands who were beginning to suffer from exposure – were taken off to hospital in ambulances. I hadn't suffered too badly and was kitted out again and sent on Survivor's Leave. I knew I'd probably bump into Bill and the DEMS gunners again, but saying goodbye to the rest of the crew was hard. The time we'd spent together and the dangers we'd shared had made us close, like a family.

I took the ferry from Belfast to Liverpool, where I arrived next morning. On my way to the dock gates I stopped at a telephone box to tell my mother I was on the way home, then boarded a tram at the Pier Head. The city had tidied up most of the damage inflicted during the great blitz of May 1941, but there were still large gaps among the buildings. The streets were busy with men from all three services, and there were many foreign uniforms to be seen as well.

It had been a while since I was last home. The tram jolted its way out of the city centre, passing the many familiar sights with which I had grown up. Liverpool was a city where every penny earned and spent came from the sea. My dad, for example, worked for the Mersey Docks and Harbour Board, and so had Dick, my elder brother. In 1939, when it was obvious war was coming, Dick and I had joined the Royal Artillery at the local

Territorial Army drill hall. Now he was a sergeant serving in Malta with a heavy anti-aircraft regiment. All the reports I heard said Malta was having a very rough time of it at the moment.

A man in a flashy suit and tie boarded the tram and sat down next to me.

'Where are you stationed?' he asked.

'I'm a gunner on a merchant ship,' I replied.

'Merchant Navy, eh? I heard a lot of blokes who should be in the Army or the Navy go in for that because it's a cushy life – regular meals, good beds, that sort of thing. Wasters like that should be thrown out and made to join up, that's what I say! I bet you've seen some of them yourself!'

It was true that at first I had wanted to serve in a field regiment and I wasn't that happy about being on a merchant ship. Sometimes, I still couldn't help myself thinking that the Merchant Navy wasn't quite the real thing. Normally I am easy going, but this guy was starting to annoy me. Before the man knew what was happening, I grabbed him by his flash tie and stared straight at him.

'Listen, you!' I said. 'The blokes I've been at

sea with bring you the food you eat! They risk being torpedoed, bombed, blown apart or burned to death to do it! They go back to sea time after time without even being asked!'

'Keep your wig on, soldier!' he said hoarsely. 'I was just being sociable, that's all!'

'And another thing,' I went on, 'if you're so keen on people joining up, why don't you do it yourself?'

'War work!' he croaked. 'Important war work! Can't talk about it!'

'You're a spiv, aren't you?' I said. 'You steal the things men risk their lives to bring here and sell them for your own profit, don't you?'

The conductor, who wore Great War medal ribbons on his uniform, tapped the spiv on the shoulder.

'You – off!' he said, pointing to the platform. 'I'm not having trouble-makers on my tram!'

To my surprise, as the red-faced spiv left, the rest of the passengers applauded. The conductor winked at me.

'Well done, lad. He's had that coming for a while.'

'It was nothing,' I said, feeling slightly ashamed because I wasn't really sure I believed what I'd said about merchant seamen.

My stop arrived and I gratefully left the tram. I walked across to our house, thinking how strange it is that after you've been away from anywhere it seems to be smaller when you get back. I rang the bell and my mother opened the door. She looked older than I remembered her, and tired.

'Hallo, our John!' she said, giving me a hug. 'You've grown a lot – but you've lost weight, too. I hope they're feeding you properly.'

'Don't worry, Mam,' I said, 'the grub's fine – until the cook gets his hands on it, that is! Tell you the truth, I think we eat better than you do when we're in foreign ports.'

She bustled about, getting together a good tea for us. Strict rationing made it difficult for her but she had a small stock of good things put by for special occasions and opened her last can of peaches. I heard the front door open and Dad walked in, back from work.

'Hallo, John lad!' he said, laughing as he shook my hand warmly. 'This is a grand surprise, and no mistake!'

'His ship's gone down,' said Mam. 'He's on

Survivor's Leave, so we'll have him for a few days yet.'

Dad nodded sympathetically.

'Bad, was it?' he asked.

'A couple of the blokes got knocked about a bit, but it could have been worse. We got the U-boat that did it, though.'

Dad chuckled.

'You never were one to let yourself get pushed around, were you, son? Ah, well, it's bad news about the *Mary Cranfield*, but you'll get another ship soon enough – the chances are she'll be an improvement.'

'How about you, Dad? Still at the Dock Board?' I asked.

'Yes, I'm in the Movements Department now. You know, finding the right dock so a ship can be loaded and unloaded quickly. Keeps me going flat out because there's so much to think about – convoys in, convoys out, tides, tugs, escorts and the rest of it. I don't mind though because it's a useful job.'

'He works too hard,' said Mam. 'When he's finished at the Dock Board he does a couple of nights a week as an air-raid warden, then there's his allotment.'

'Aye, I grow most of our own vegetables now. You've just had some of them.'

'How's the leg standing up to all this, Dad?' I asked.

He grimaced.

'Gives me trouble now and again. Like I said back in 1918, "You should have given me a wooden one – you know where you stand with them!"'

We both roared with laughter.

'What's the news from Dick?' I asked.

Dad's face suddenly became serious.

'So far as we know, he's all right,' he said. 'He doesn't say much in his letters and we don't know anyone who can tell us what's going on in Malta these days. But with the Luftwaffe and the Italians doing everything they can to flatten that little island, and him in the middle of it all, your Mam's worried sick, though she tries not to show it.'

'You'll be told soon enough if anything bad happens to him,' I said. 'No news really is good news, you know.'

They showed me the most recent letters they had received from Dick. He didn't seem to write often, or maybe his letters just weren't getting through. He wrote about incessant air raids and how bravely the Maltese were standing up to the ordeal, but not much else. The three of us talked, then listened to the news on the wireless. I was tired from all the travelling though and turned in early. Despite the tiredness, I couldn't sleep. It was too quiet. There was the sound of traffic and tramcars on the road outside, of course, but something was absent. It was the steady thump-thump-thump of the *Mary Cranfield*'s engines. Suddenly I realized how much I would miss her.

The next morning, after Dad had left for work, I was having breakfast when the doorbell rang. My mother answered it and a minute later she came into the kitchen, trembling and ashen-faced, holding a telegram.

'You open it,' she said in a whisper. 'I can't.'

Chapter 3
The *Ohio*

Telegrams were almost always bad news. They usually meant that someone had been killed, wounded or was missing in action, and I knew Mam was thinking of Dick. I looked at the envelope.

'It's all right,' I said. 'It's for me.'

Her face relaxed with relief.

The telegram read:

LEAVE CANCELLED STOP JOIN MV OHIO GREENOCK IMMEDIATELY STOP RTO LIME STREET WILL ISSUE RAIL WARRANT ON PRODUCTION OF THIS ORDER STOP

Needless to say, I wasn't pleased, but I put the best face possible on it.

'Sorry, Mam,' I said, 'I'm wanted. They just can't get along without me!'

So, reluctantly and without having had

time to rest, I was off to war again. I got my kit together and was ready to leave within ten minutes. I knew saying goodbye to Mam again would be difficult.

'Say goodbye to Dad for me, will you, Mam?' I said as we stood by the front door. My mother belonged to the old school who believe in keeping a stiff upper lip and I knew she wouldn't shed a tear until the door had closed behind me, then she'd let go.

'Look after yourself, son,' she said. 'I'll just keep praying all of this will be over soon.'

'You and me both, Mam.' I chucked her under the chin. She said it was cheeky, but it always made her laugh.

'There's better times ahead, eh? Don't fret, I'll write when I can.'

I reported to the Routing and Transport Officer (RTO) at Lime Street Station. Bill, Ron and the rest of the DEMS gunners from the *Mary Cranfield* were there, looking equally fed up and bewildered. When we arrived at Greenock in Scotland, I met several more DEMS gunners under a Bombardier Labarn, who, being senior to Bill, would command the combined detachment. To my surprise, we were joined by a number of naval ratings under a petty officer named Jack Holder, a big bluff, no-nonsense regular. The local RTO arranged for a launch to ferry us all out to our new ship, the *Ohio*.

On the journey over, Jack Holder came over to our small group.

'You're the ship's DEMS gunners, right?' He asked Bill.

'That's right. What about you?' Bill replied.

'Seems they couldn't round up enough of you, so we're along to help out. We're all anti-aircraft gunners.'

'I didn't think any merchant ship carried AA guns.'

'This one does. She's an American tanker, but she's got a new all-British crew from the Eagle Oil Company. Special arrangement between the Ministry of War Transport and the American government. Built a year or two back and they say she's the best.'

'That's strange,' said Bill. 'Why should the Americans hand over a good tanker and beach their own crew?'

'Search me, chum. I'm just telling you what I've heard. To my mind we're in for something special – and that means dangerous.'

'Any idea where we're going?'

Jack laughed.

'Now, if we'd been issued with tropical gear I'd say Russia, and if we'd got Arctic clothing I'd say the tropics. That's how the Navy works. But as we've got neither, your guess is as good as mine!'

The coxswain cut the launch's motor as we closed in on the *Ohio*. She had not yet taken on her cargo of oil and so she towered over us. I gasped in awe. She must have been at least 500 feet long! With the setting sun tinting her grey paintwork a rosy pink above the dark waters of the Clyde, she was an impressive and imposing sight.

Once aboard, I was shown to my quarters. They were the ultimate in luxury compared to what I'd been used to aboard the old *Mary Cranfield*, and far better than anything you'd have found on most British merchantmen. Having unpacked my kit, I met the others in the mess hall. The cooks told us that the Americans had generously left the pantry full of things that hadn't been seen for years. Our first meal consisted of as much steak as we wanted, with a dozen brands of sauce, followed by strawberries and ice-cream. It was heaven!

Over the next few days I began to recognize the ship's officers. Captain Dudley Mason was dark and had a long face with intelligent, humorous eyes and a determined chin. He seemed to take great pride in his crew. Someone told me he came from down south, a place called Surbiton in Surrey. The watch-keeping officers, including Gray, the first officer, McKilligan, the second mate, and Stephen, third mate, were all quietly spoken Scots. The chief engineer, James Wyld, was an old shipmate of the skipper's; the second was a Cornishman named Buddle, the third, a big South African called Grinstead. There were also several junior officers and cadets.

Now, I was brought up to believe that, no matter what the uniform is or the number of rings on the sleeve, the man inside should have your respect only if he's earned it. It's got me into trouble for speaking my mind more than once. Leadership is something you can't describe, but you know instinctively when someone has got it, and when I learned that these men were the pick of the Eagle fleet it didn't surprise me. I couldn't avoid comparing their youth and quiet, confident efficiency with the *Mary Cranfield*'s old worn-out officers. The *Ohio* and her crew represented the Merchant Navy at its best.

On the first morning, with the chief engineer's permission, the gun crews toured the engine room. There was a lot of work going on. One of the engineers explained that earlier in the year another tanker had been lost when the shock wave from a near miss severed a vital steam pipe, leaving her a sitting duck. To reduce the risk of this happening again, they were installing rubber bearings beneath the *Ohio*'s engines, with every steam pipe supported by steel springs and balks of timber. They were certainly taking a lot of trouble with the *Ohio* and it made me wonder again just what our mission was.

That afternoon Bill, Ron and I were on the poop with the rest of the 5-inch gun crew, putting the gun into working order. I was stripping down the breech when one of the ship's officers strolled up. He looked about my age and from the one ring on the arm of his jacket I could see that he was a junior officer.

'Aye, aye,' I said. 'All right?'

'G'day, how goes it with the artillery?'

The voice was unmistakably Australian.

'You from down under?' I asked.

'Yeah, how d'ya guess?'

He told us that he had been to school at an Australian training ship then come to London, where Eagle Oil had accepted him as a cadet just before the outbreak of war.

'I expected to do four years' sea service before I got my first ring,' he said. 'Time at the training ship cut that a bit, as did the war, so here I am – Junior Officer Bruce Cameron, at your service.'

'What's your job aboard, then?' I asked.

'Well, I've still some exams to take before I can stand watches alone, so for the moment I stand 'em with the first officer. My other job is looking after the cadets, so I'm a bit of a spare part really. Anyway, how about you? How d'you like being a DEMS gunner?'

I shrugged.

'Being a gunner is fine, though I'd rather be with a field regiment ashore than on merchant ships. Still, you take what you're given and this ship seems all right.'

'Ever serve on tankers before?'

I shook my head.

31

'First time. I'm in two minds about it. Before, I only stood a chance of being drowned – now I can be blown to bits as well!'

'Pity you're not a member of the crew. We get a shilling a day danger money,' he said with a wry smile.

'What – seven bob a week! Oh, yes, that's well worth risking your life for!'

We both laughed.

Bill Ryan came bustling up, very much the gun commander.

'Is this man bothering you, sir?' he said to Bruce, then turned to me. 'Haven't you stripped that firing assembly yet?'

'This is Bombardier Ryan,' I said. 'He's been following me around since before Dunkirk. Can't get rid of him!'

'Any more cheek out of you, young feller, and you'll be back on muzzle loaders!' said Bill with mock ferocity. 'Thinks he knows it all because he's been shipwrecked! Any idea where we're going, sir?'

'Nah.' Bruce shook his head. 'Even the skipper's in the dark. Reckon we're in for something pretty big, though.'

We chatted for a few minutes longer before Bruce went on his way. After that, things began to move very quickly. We went down to Dunglass and took on over 11,000 tons of diesel fuel oil and kerosene. Lieutenant Denys Barton, the naval liaison officer who was to accompany us, came aboard. The anchorage in the Clyde began filling up and it became obvious that a convoy and its escort were assembling.

The merchant vessels, I noticed, were all fast, modern ships, although from a distance their wartime grey paint obscured which shipping lines they belonged to. The day after we arrived at Dunglass, Barton and the skipper left the *Ohio* to board a cruiser for the convoy conference. As tradition demanded of a civilian master, Captain Mason wore a lounge suit, trilby hat and well-shined shoes. The whole crew were anxious to know where we were going and eagerly awaited some news. When he did return the word went round the ship in five minutes that we were bound for Malta – the most dangerous island in the Mediterranean.

Shortly after, an announcement was made over the public-address system and all hands were summoned to the crew mess hall. Once assembled, Captain Mason read the sealed orders confirming our destination and told us that the Royal Navy would do everything in its power to get us there. He also told us what to expect.

'The good news is that the Eighth Army has halted the advance of Rommel and his Afrika Korps at a place called El Alamein,' he said. 'Our aircraft and submarines from Malta are playing havoc with his supply lines. That counts for a lot because when the Eighth Army counter-attacks it stands a good chance of throwing him out of Egypt.'

There was a murmur of approval.

'Now for the difficult part,' he continued. 'Malta is rapidly running out of everything – anti-aircraft ammunition, fuel of every kind, food and kerosene for cooking. Worse still, every recent attempt to re-supply the island has failed, with heavy loss of merchant shipping. That is why we are part of a fast, heavily escorted convoy. We've got to get through. If we don't, Malta will be forced to surrender within a month and the war in Africa will take a turn for the worse.

'It won't be easy. The enemy will do everything in his power to stop us. He's got plenty of submarines and torpedo boats, and we'll be under attack as soon as we're within flying range of Sardinia. There's also the possibility that the Italian surface fleet will come out after us. It's only right you should know what we're up against.'

I glanced around the hall and saw the serious looks on everyone's faces. I don't think any of us had been expecting a mission as dangerous as this one.

'You men have been specifically chosen for this voyage,' Mason went on. 'You probably wouldn't choose it yourself, but just remember you are chosen men. I want no dodgers, no questions asked when an order is given. If you are called upon to do extra duties, just remember that this is a special trip and one of enormous importance. I don't expect it's going to be a picnic, but just look outside and see the sort of escort we've got. I've no doubt whatsoever that you will keep up the traditions of the Merchant Service. I have the utmost confidence in you all.'

While he was speaking the mood in the mess hall had become one of grim, silent realism, but the men gave him a cheer when he had finished.

'We'll get you there, sir,' the boatswain said. 'Right, lads?'

There was a murmur of assent in which I

heard myself joining. After all, I now had a real stake in the success of the voyage because of my brother, Dick. While the captain was talking I had felt a sudden chill of fear on his account. What would happen if we were sunk on the way, or arrived too late? Would the enemy follow up his air attacks with an invasion of Malta while we were on passage? If Dick survived, the best he could expect was to be shipped off to a prison camp. The mission had to succeed.

I went on deck to do some thinking. I leaned against the 5-inch gun, watching the convoy form up in the dusk. The *Ohio* had more guns than I'd ever seen on a merchant ship and now I knew why. There was a 40-mm Bofors anti-aircraft gun on a platform just above and forward of where I was standing, and I knew there was a 3-inch anti-aircraft gun up on the bows, plus six Oerlikon cannons and three half-inch Browning heavy machine-guns at various points around the upper deck. Before me was the largest group of escort vessels I'd ever encountered.

The plating began to vibrate, telling me that the main engines were turning. I heard the sound of quietly spoken orders and the rattle as the anchor chain came in. Now I could see foam beneath the stern as the *Ohio* began to move forward. Tugs hooted and destroyers gave their distinctive whoop-whoop as the great mass of ships took up their positions. There would be no stopping now until we reached Malta.

Chapter 4
Convoy

We were off the Portuguese coast. The day was fine, the sea was calm and visibility was good. The convoy, consisting of fourteen merchant vessels in three columns, was pushing steadily south at a good 15 knots. That might not sound very fast, but the speed of a convoy is that of its slowest ship, and I'd been used to slopping along at 7 or 8 knots. Usually, we steered a zigzag course to put the U-boats off their aim, but we weren't doing much of that just now. Instead, the convoy commodore was exercising the ships in other ways, such as altering formation, increasing or reducing speed and making emergency turns.

It all required intense concentration on the part of the ships' officers and I could understand why. Changing direction suddenly at

15 knots increases the chances of dangerous collisions between ships that aren't used to working together. And as far as the *Ohio* was concerned, she displaced about 30,000 tons when fully laden and you can just imagine the time it takes to haul that amount of dead weight off a straight line.

What surprised me most, though, was the size of the escort. There, in the distance, I saw the unmistakable shapes of the battleships *Nelson* and *Rodney*, great mountains of armour plate easily identified by their three, triple 16-inch gun turrets mounted forward. There were also a number of fast and powerful-looking cruisers and more destroyers than I could count, dashing here and there. We seemed to be enclosed in a ring of steel and it was very reassuring.

I was stacking 5-inch shells in the ready-use locker beside the gun when Lieutenant Barton, the smart, clean-cut naval liaison officer, came along. Bill saluted him and pointed to the warships.

'Not much chance our little pop-gun here will be needed with all that fire-power about, sir,' he said, patting the barrel.

'I think you're right, Bombardier,' Barton replied. 'We can take care of anything on the surface, but I'm a little concerned about the anti-aircraft side of things.'

The whole gun crew exchanged glances in surprise when we heard this, but Bill said nothing and the officer continued.

'I've just come from an anti-aircraft cruiser in the eastern Mediterranean. Despite the number of AA guns we're carrying, *Ohio*'s problem is that we haven't got enough trained crew to man all the guns, even with the extra naval ratings aboard. To solve the problem, Captain Mason has detailed his cadets to receive instruction in handling the weapons.'

'The cadets, sir? I thought all the Merchant Navy blokes were classed as non-combatants,' said Bill.

'Quite right, Bombardier,' Barton replied, 'but I think we can take the broad view that if they're attacked they are entitled to defend themselves. However, that still leaves us short, so as we agree that the five-inch is unlikely to be used, I'd like you and your gun crew to join them. That way you'll be able to handle the AA armament or the five-inch as the situation demands.'

'Sounds all right to me,' said Bill. 'Just one point, though, sir – who's going to look after the ammunition supply for the automatic weapons?'

'That's taken care of. Captain Mason has detailed ammunition parties from the crew. They'll be on stand-by day and night. Once you've finished stowing you'll find Petty Officer Holder running the cadets' class amidships.' And with that Barton walked away.

'The Merchant Navy manning guns, whatever next?' commented Bill.

When we had finished stowing the shells, Bill, Ron and I walked forward of the bridge island to find Jack Holder. He was a big man with a big voice to match. He was a forceful instructor who could be heard all over the ship. When we arrived he was laying into a pink-faced cadet.

'I won't tell you again!' he shouted. 'If you put your fingers near the breech-block when the weapon is in action, the next you'll see of them will be coming out of the barrel! Understand?'

Like other instructors I'd trained under, he seemed to motivate men by shouting at their mistakes, then making them feel great with praise and encouragement once they started getting things right.

The cadets were nearing the end of the instruction period and were clearly enjoying the break from their usual routine. Holder turned to Bruce Cameron, who was watching over the men, deadly serious beneath his smile.

'Mr Cameron, sir, if you've any influence with the engine room I'd be glad if you'd get them to weld stops on these mountings. We don't want your young gentlemen firing inboard when they get excited, do we, now?'

The idea of Browning or Oerlikon rounds flying round the *Ohio*'s decks was just too hair-raising to think about. Bruce gave his crooked Australian grin and pushed his cap on to the back of his head.

'Yeah, fair go – I'll see to it.'

Most of the gunners had some experience of automatic weapons, and although these were bigger than anything we'd handled before the principles were the same. Holder took us through the loading and firing drill, then went on to demonstrate stripping and cleaning. 'What's the Oerlikon's rate of fire?' I asked.

'In theory, it's about 450 rounds a minute,' said Holder. 'We'll be using magazines, though, so it will be a lot less – apart from

42

which, you'll be firing short, aimed bursts until you know you're on target.'

I pointed to the sights above the gun. They consisted of a series of wire circles surrounding a central aiming mark.

'How do we use these?'

'If the enemy is coming towards you, aim above him; if he's going away, aim below; if he's flying parallel, aim ahead; likewise if he's diving on you. Watch your tracer, and once you see it going in, keep at him. Common sense, really.'

'What kind of ammunition are we using?' asked Bill.

'There's tracer, of course, then armour-piercing, incendiary and fragmentation. The incendiary starts fires, the fragmentation blows itself apart when it hits – can cause a lot of damage. No need for you to worry about it – it's all loaded in sequence in the magazines.'

When we got back to the 5-inch the crew manning the Bofors were grinning down at us from their mounting. They hadn't been with us aboard the *Mary Cranfield* but they were a cheery lot and had managed to get out of Dunkirk as a team. Just for the moment, they were the professionals and we were the amateurs.

'Hey, Bom!' one of them shouted at Bill. 'That right you're doing anti-aircraft defence now? If so, can we have a posting ashore when we get to Gibraltar?'

'And when did you lot last hit anything?' Bill shouted back. 'If you're as good as you think you are, I want half-a-dozen downed enemy aircraft from each of you before we get to Malta!'

After breakfast next morning I went up on deck. The atmosphere was very tense and I could tell that everyone was waiting nervously for the enemy's first appearance. Visibility was poor because of fog and low cloud. We could hear an aircraft circling the convoy and, thinking it might be a Condor, everyone went to action stations. As the aircraft broke cloud the entire escort erupted in a blaze of anti-aircraft fire which stopped almost as soon as it had begun. To our horror we saw that the aircraft was a Sunderland which had probably been engaged in an anti-submarine patrol for our protection.

Badly hit, the huge flying boat plunged into the sea and sank at once. The destroyer *Ledbury* raced to the scene. I saw several of her lads going over the side to help without a moment's hesitation, but they managed to bring out only one man alive. I felt totally shocked by what I had just seen.

'That's a rotten way to go,' I said.

'I'm sorry for the gunners that did it, too,' replied Ron. 'They'll never forgive themselves for that.'

'Listen, you lot!' Bill snapped. 'In war, accidents happen and people get killed because of them. Get used to the idea. Now there's a lesson for us in this: in action, when you're tracking your target, make damn sure you don't hit any other ships, or you'll be the ones killing your own people.'

It was a harsh view but, of course, Bill was right.

The further south we went, the warmer it got. One day I was standing by the rail looking at the other merchantmen in the convoy. I was certain I'd seen several of them on the Mersey at one time or another, so when Bruce Cameron walked past I asked him about them.

'Yeah, they'll be the *Melbourne Star* and the *Brisbane Star* – a couple of Blue Star's cargo liners,' he said. 'You've probably seen Blue Funnel's *Deucalion* as well.'

He pointed out the rest of the ships.

'*Empire Hope, Wairangi* and *Waimarama* all belong to Shaw Saville. They're cargo and passenger, built for the South African run, and they really are fast – if anything, we're holding them back. There's *Rochester Castle* from the Union Castle Line – she was on the South African run, too. The rest of them are *Dorset, Glenorchy, Port Chalmers* and *Clan Ferguson*. Those two over there are the *Santa Elisa* and the *Almeria Lykes* – American-owned, brand, spanking new and under charter to the Ministry. They've still got their American crews, too – that's why they're flying the Stars and Stripes.'

'What are they all carrying?' I asked.

'They're all loaded with flour and other foodstuffs, ammunition, and some cased petrol and aviation spirit in jerricans,' he said. 'The idea is that if only a few of them get through, they'll deliver enough of each to keep Malta going.'

I was horrified. Even in smaller quantities cased petrol was a far more dangerous cargo than the fuel oil and kerosene we were carrying.

'Petrol! That's a bit risky, isn't it? I thought we were the only travelling bomb in the convoy!'

Suddenly Bruce's expression was serious and for the first time I began to see the ship's officer beneath his friendly exterior.

'This whole thing's a risk,' he said. 'We're all going to have to take our chances in our different ways. Like you said when you came aboard, you don't have a choice so you take what you're given.'

I nodded.

'By the way,' he added, 'did you know the convoy's been given a name? It's Pedestal.'

'I wonder who thought that one up – still, it's as good as anything else,' I said.

Later that day, just before dusk, we turned east to enter the Straits of Gibraltar. There the escort was reinforced with yet more cruisers and destroyers and, best of all, the four aircraft carriers *Eagle*, *Indomitable*, *Victorious* and *Furious*. The last, we learned, would be accompanying us only until she was able to fly off thirty-eight Spitfires to reinforce the RAF on Malta, but the others would provide us with fighter defence against air attack.

We slid past the Rock, its reassuring bulk black against the darkening sky. The whole sea seemed to be covered with warships. It was a sight which encouraged us all.

'Can't see how we can possibly fail with this lot to see us through!' said Ron.

'I wondered whether we'd reach Malta when we left the Clyde,' I said. 'Now I'm sure we will.'

Bill was staring grimly at the receding lights along the Spanish coastline.

'Don't get cocky, sunshine!' he said sharply. 'That's Spain over there. It's run by General Franco, who just happens to be one of Adolf Hitler's best mates. By now, details of every ship will be on their way to Berlin and Rome, and you can bet your boots they've a fair idea what we're up to. Take it from me, they'll be waiting for us!'

Chapter 5
First Blood

It was the morning of 11 August and we were steaming in four columns across the western Mediterranean on a fine day that promised to be hot. The carriers were flying off their aircraft, some to form defensive patrols above the convoy, others on missions far beyond the horizon. We tracked them with our anti-aircraft guns, just for practice, under the watchful eye of Petty Officer Holder. Handling an Oerlikon wasn't as easy as it looked, but gradually I got used to it and after a couple of hours I was able to keep an aircraft where I wanted it in the ring sight.

While we were doing this, the crew's ammunition parties also practised their drill. We got on well with them and they were really keen. One of the engineering staff, a pumpman called Collins, even rigged up a hoist so that the Bofors crew could have a regular supply of shells; as it looked like a gallows, we started calling him The Hangman.

It really was a perfect morning and I had started to relax a little. Just after midday I was going through the motions of changing a magazine when there was a sudden heavy explosion to starboard and astern. I glanced up to see a huge column of dirty brown water rising beside the aircraft-carrier *Eagle*. Then, at two-second intervals, there came three more explosions and more columns of water were thrown skywards. It was what we all dreaded: an undetected U-boat attack.

I watched as the carrier slowed rapidly and took on a heavy list to port. I could see the tiny, ant-like figures of her crew running down the tilting flight deck and jumping into the sea. Then, all hell broke loose. With their sirens whoop-whooping, destroyers closed in to depth-charge the surrounding area and pick up survivors. The convoy itself made an emergency turn to port. I scrambled around, looking for life-jackets and anything else that might be useful, but we were too far away to help. To my horror, just eight minutes after the U-boat's torpedoes had struck her, the

Eagle had gone, leaving a spreading area of oil and flotsam to mark where she had been.

I was shocked that our first contact with the enemy had been so sudden and without warning, and also that such a fine old carrier, such a large ship, could meet such a quick end. Four of her aircraft, which were airborne at the time, landed on other carriers, but the rest were lost with her. It was a sobering thought when I realized that in so short a time we had lost about one-third of our fighter cover. You couldn't include the *Furious* because, shortly after the *Eagle* went down, she began flying off her Spitfires on their one-way flight to Malta, now less than 500 miles distant. We didn't mind that so much though, because we knew we'd have their protection again once we neared the end of our voyage. Even so, when the carrier completed her mission and turned back to Gibraltar with her escort, we felt a further sense of loss.

During the afternoon the destroyers depth-charged every likely contact spotted by their submarine-detection equipment. This foiled several attacks and kept the enemy at a distance. We also heard that on their way back one of *Furious*'s escorts, the destroyer

Wolverine, had rammed and sunk the Italian submarine *Dagabur*. That brought us some satisfaction.

After the morning's events, I was prepared for enemy attack and when, later in the afternoon, the alarm klaxon sounded Action Stations, I eagerly grabbed my steel helmet and ran to the gun. I couldn't see anything with the naked eye – the raider was too high – but the word was that the fleet radar had identified a high-altitude reconnaissance aircraft. The two battleships' heavy anti-aircraft guns – the only weapons capable of reaching that height – went into action, without result. The pilot must have successfully done his job of reporting our position because at dusk the enemy made his first real air attack.

I could see them approaching from the direction of Sardinia, little black dots that grew larger until they could be identified as Junkers Ju-88 dive-bombers and Heinkel He-111s with torpedoes, thirty-six of them in all, flying at about 5,000 feet. The Junkers came in first in a long, steady dive. Then, quite suddenly, the carriers' fighters were swooping down on them from above and behind, machine-guns blazing. Several of the enemy, trailing smoke and flames, reeled out of their formation to smash into the sea. The remainder came on but were clearly shaken as our anti-aircraft barrage went up, filling the entire sky with tracer from escorts and merchantmen alike. Swerving to avoid the worst of it, the enemy planes bombed wildly and hit nothing.

What with the roar of aero engines, bombs exploding and guns of every size firing as fast as they could, the noise level was deafening. I saw the tracers from my Oerlikon rip into the belly of a Junkers that flew directly overhead, but then the magazine ran out and by the time it was changed he had disappeared. I heard someone shout that he'd gone into the sea about 400 yards off the starboard side, but I could hardly claim it for myself as so many others had also been firing at it.

More of the Junkers were hit, either passing overhead to plunge into the sea or wheeling away in the direction of home, trailing smoke. The Heinkels, now under attack from the fighters, hadn't liked what they'd seen. I saw them release their torpedoes a long way out, then clear off without waiting to see the results. The ships simply made an emergency turn towards them and the torpedoes ran harmlessly between the lines.

As suddenly as it had started, it was all over. In rotation, the fighters came in to make a dusk landing on the carriers. The cadets manning the nearest Browning were jumping up and down, cheering and shouting as though they'd shot down half the Luftwaffe. Gray, the first officer, appeared on the bridge, looking annoyed.

'Mr Cameron,' he shouted at Bruce, 'get your people back under control – *now*!'

'Aye aye, sir!' said Bruce. 'All right, fellers, give it a rest, will ya! There'll be plenty to celebrate when we reach Malta – right now, we're just getting started!'

It would be wrong to say we went to bed well satisfied that night, because we didn't go to bed at all. Instead, we stretched out by the guns. Although an air attack seemed unlikely after dark, by now the risk from submarines and motor torpedo boats was always present and so we took it in turns to stand watch, keeping the guns loaded and ready. It was too hot to sleep below decks, anyway. The cooks brought our grub round and we talked over the day's events.

The *Eagle*'s loss saddened us, of course, but on balance we didn't think we'd done too badly during our first day's real fighting.

'I wonder how many of their planes were shot down,' mused Ron.

'Mr Barton says four for certain,' replied Bill. 'A few more were so badly damaged they'll not make it back to base.'

'How long before we get to Malta?' I asked.

'Oh, two days' steady steaming, perhaps – three, more likely. If they're all like today, then I think we stand a fair chance.'

I began to wonder. We'd hit back hard, for sure, but the enemy certainly wouldn't let it rest at that. Whether we got through would depend on what else he had in store for us.

Chapter 6
Jaws of Death

On the morning of Wednesday 12 August we stood to our guns before it was properly light. Dawn was the time when it seemed likely that the enemy would mount another air attack, hoping to catch us before we were fully awake. Aboard the carriers the fighters were beginning to take off in readiness.

Sure enough, just as I was enjoying breakfast, which consisted of a bacon sandwich and a mug of char, the alarm klaxon sounded. The enemy's reconnaissance aircraft were shadowing us again, but this time we were ready for them. From far above came the sound of machine-gun fire as the fighters went into action. In the distance, I saw two of their opponents plummet into the sea from a great height.

At 09.05 the first air attack came in. It was

a repeat of the previous day's, but this time there were fewer aircraft. Our Hurricanes and Martlets had the height advantage and they came swooping down out of the sun before the enemy knew what had hit them. The result was catastrophic. I saw eight of the Ju-88s go down for certain, and more were damaged. Very few of the remaining planes were willing to brave the anti-aircraft barrage, so those bombs that were dropped fell wide. I reckoned maybe half the attackers made it back to their base.

We steamed on. Throughout the morning the destroyers depth-charged every likely contact again, keeping the enemy submarines at bay. Shortly after midday there was another air attack. This time it was a big one, about 100 aircraft all told. First to appear were ten Italian, three-engined Savoia-Marchetti torpedo-bombers, escorted by Macchi fighters. While both sets of fighters became involved in dogfights, several of the torpedo-bombers broke through. I cocked the gun, released the safety-catch and lined up on my target. We opened up with everything we'd got.

Unwilling to penetrate the inferno of anti-aircraft fire, the bombers dropped their loads well ahead of the convoy. To my surprise, long cylinders dangling from parachutes began drifting down. As soon as they hit the water some of them exploded.

'What's going on?' I asked Bill.

'Parachute mines, maybe,' he replied. 'Looks like mines up ahead, sir!' he shouted to Lieutenant Barton, up on the bridge.

'They're circling torpedoes,' Barton shouted back. 'We've known about them for a while – they call them *motobombas*. They'd be quite dangerous if they hadn't dropped them so far out.'

At that point the convoy and escort made an emergency turn away from the danger zone. Minutes later I could see about twenty more torpedo-bombers approaching the convoy's starboard bow, with a much larger group coming to port. The usual defence against a torpedo attack is to turn towards it so that you present the smallest possible target. This time, it didn't matter which way we turned, we would still be exposing the full length of our hulls to one or other of the attacks.

'This lot know what they're doing!' exclaimed Bill in alarm. 'Keep firing, even if they are still out of range!'

The Oerlikon shook as I fired burst after burst, keeping one particular aircraft in my ring sight. I knew I was falling short, but so was every gunner in the fleet, because I could see the curtain of splashes where our rounds were falling. Our only hope was that they'd fly on into the wall of tracer that was rising in front of them.

Suddenly, there was a tremendous thunderclap from astern. I glanced round to see an immense cloud of smoke spreading around *Rodney*. She had gone into action with her 16-inch guns, firing air-bursts. When these exploded among the attacking planes, they created an area of blast and deadly, flying shell splinters several hundred yards across. Already confronted by our wall of tracer, this proved too much for the Italian pilots. They dropped their torpedoes well before their effective range and turned for home. Far ahead of the convoy, the torpedoes criss-crossed each other harmlessly. I sighed with relief and rested my head against the gun. These constant attacks were exhausting.

We were still congratulating ourselves on another escape when Mr Barton shouted down to us from the bridge that a high-level attack was coming in. Looking up, I saw twenty or so specks that rapidly grew into the ugly gull-winged shape of Junkers Ju-87 vertical dive-bombers, otherwise known as Stukas. Then, rising in intensity as they gathered speed, we heard their sirens howling. The sound went right through me and made my skin crawl.

'These are the real pros,' said Bill as they bore down on us. 'They're anti-shipping specialists – gave the Royal Navy a hard time off Crete last year.'

The sky was suddenly covered with the brown puffs of bursting shells. One after another, the Stukas came boring straight down, ignoring the flak as though it wasn't there. For some reason they concentrated most of their attention on the two battleships and the anti-aircraft cruiser *Cairo*, which were surrounded by huge fountains of water thrown up by exploding bombs. Everyone was firing. From forward I could hear the naval gunners banging off their 3-inch as fast as they could go, from aft came the steady thump-thump-thump-thump of the Bofors, and from everywhere else came the rattling bursts of Oerlikons and Brownings.

I developed the technique of allowing an

aircraft to enter the ring sight then, without changing the point of aim, firing a longer burst so that it simply flew into it. In this way I saw my tracer stitching its way along the engine cowling of a Stuka diving on the *Cairo*. The aircraft released its bombs, which fell astern, then banked heavily away, trailing smoke. As the gun started to overheat it became less accurate and began to suffer stoppages. But suddenly the Stukas had gone, those that survived jinking and flying low over the water. Most gunners were compelled to cease firing to avoid hitting other ships, so only the destroyers on the outer screen were able to keep their guns in action until the enemy were out of range.

I looked at the Stukas, now fast-diminishing specks on the horizon.

'You couldn't fight your way out of a wet newspaper!' I said, more or less to myself, 'You can't beat us, so don't bother trying!'

It was false bravado really, though. I was shaking with nerves and adrenalin. The truth was I was terrified but my training and the thought of Dick kept me going.

'Stop chuntering like an old woman and change that barrel before it melts!' shouted Bill angrily.

As I tried to calm down and started to change the barrel, I watched our fighters returning to the carrier. Something looked odd about the last two planes. Then I gasped in disbelief. Two of the Italian fighter-bombers had tagged on behind the Hurricanes coming in to land on *Victorious*. They looked a lot like Hurricanes and the gunners obviously took them to be friendly. At this point they opened their throttles and flashed along the flight deck, which was crowded with aircraft waiting to be taken down below, dropping a bomb each. One hit the deck but mercifully did not explode, while the other went over the bows. Jinking to avoid vengeful fire, the planes sped off to the north.

'Cheeky blighters!' shouted Bruce from a nearby Browning. 'Got away with it, too!'

I don't think any of us could quite believe it. But in a strange way, I was glad they'd got away unharmed. If they'd been our blokes pulling a stroke like that on the enemy, you'd say they deserved a slice of luck. The general opinion was that the Italians weren't very interested in the war. Well, that may be true of some of them, but there were others who really knew their business and were as brave as anyone you could meet. We'd just witnessed proof of that.

The ship's Tannoy crackled into life.

'D'ye hear there!' It was Mr Barton, apparently still thinking he was aboard a warship. 'Here are the results of the last raid . . .' He might have been talking about a football match. 'Our fighters shot down nine of the enemy, and the ships another two. We believe several more are too badly damaged to reach their base. Well done, everyone.'

We all cheered. Then I noticed the *Deucalion*. She had been leading the convoy's port column, but had now swung out of line and was slowing. I heard someone say that she'd been near-missed several times. It was an uncanny reminder of what had happened to the *Mary Cranfield* less than a month ago, although it seemed much longer. She dropped steadily astern until she disappeared below the western horizon. An hour or so later a column of smoke appeared in that direction, followed by the flashes of several heavy explosions.

'That sounds bad,' I said.

Ron, who was standing near me, nodded grimly.

'I think that's the last we'll see of her,' he replied.

Suddenly I felt the adrenalin drain out of me. I sat down heavily on the deck. I realized how impossible our mission was and for the first time wondered how much more we could take.

THE SHIPS OF THE PEDESTAL CONVOY

Destroyers

HMS *Ledbury*

Specification

Class: Hunt Class escort destroyer
Tonnage: 1,250
Maximum speed: 25 Knots
Armament: 4 x 4 in AA
              4 x 2 pdr AA
              2-3 x 20 mm AA
Commander: Lieutenant Commander RP Hill

Part of close escort that turned back to Gibraltar.

HMS *Penn*

Specification
Class: P Class destroyer
Tonnage: 1,540
Maximum speed: 36 knots
Armament: 4 x 4.7 in guns
        4 x 2 pdr AA
        8 x 20 mm AA
        8 x 21 in torpedo tubes
Commander: Lieutenant Commander Swaine

Part of close escort that turned back to
Gibraltar.

Aircraft Carriers

HMS *Eagle*

Specification
```
Tonnage: 10,850
Maximum speed: 25 knots
Armour:    main belt 2-3 in
           deck 1 in
Armament:  6 x 5.5 in guns
           3 x 4 in AA
           8 x 2 pdr AA
           16 x 20 mm AA
Aircraft: 20
Complement: 664 (excluding aircrew)
```

Torpedoed by U-73 on 11 August and sunk.
16 Aircraft lost.

HMS *Indomitable*

Specification

Class: Illustrious Class aircraft carrier

Tonnage: 23,000

Maximum speed: 31 knots

Armour: main belt 4$\frac{1}{2}$ in
               hanger side 4$\frac{1}{2}$ in
               deck 2$\frac{1}{2}$-3 in

Armament: 16 x 4.5 in dual purpose
               48 x 2 pdr AA
               38 x 20 mm AA

Aircraft: 36

Complement: 1,392

Bomb damage on 12 August. Part of escort that turned back to Gibraltar.

Anti-aircraft cruiser
HMS *Cairo*

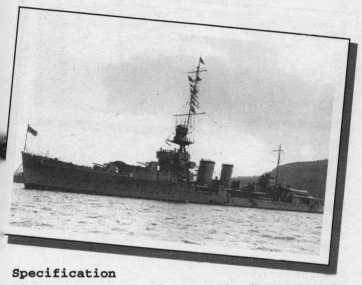

Specification

Class: Cape Town Class anti-aircraft cruiser

Tonnage: 4,290

Maximum speed: 29 knots

Armour: main belt 1¼–2¼ in
           midships 3 in
           aft 2–2½ in
           deck 1 in

Armament: 8 x 4 in AA
          4 x 2 pdr AA
          8 x .50 in AA

Complement: 400

Torpedoed by Italian submarine *Axum* on 12 August and sunk.

Cargo Ships

Brisbane Star

Specification
Gross registered tonnage: 12,791
Owners: Blue Star Line
Captain: Captain Riley

Arrived at Malta with bomb and torpedo damage.

Melbourne Star

Specification
Gross registered tonnage: 12,806
Owners: Blue Star Line
Captain: Captain Macfarlane

Arrived at Malta with bomb damage.

Port Chalmers

Specification
Gross registered tonnage: 8,535
Owners: Port Line
Captain: Captain Pinkey

Arrived at Malta with bomb damage.

Rochester Castle

Specification
Gross registered tonnage: 7,795
Owners: Union Castle
Captain: Captain Richard Wren

Arrived at Malta with bomb and torpedo
damage.

Tanker
Ohio

Specification

Built for Texaco, under charter to the
Ministry of War Transport.

Manned by British crew provided by Eagle
Oil and Shipping Company.

Captain: Captain Dudley Mason

Capacity: 12,500 tons fuel oil

Armament: 1 x 5 in gun
          1 x 3 in AA
          1 x 40 mm Bofors AA
          3 x .50 in AA
          6 x 20 mm Oerlikon AA

Chapter 7
Fighting Through

The afternoon wore on and the depth-charging continued. I was still at my gun because enemy aircraft kept snooping about, so the cooks came round again with char and sandwiches. It was about 16.15 when the depth-charging suddenly intensified. Twenty minutes later a submarine brokc surface in a flurry of foam. Two destroyers closed in, guns blazing. At full speed, one of them rammed her with a crash of tearing metal we could hear a mile away. A lot of the crew managed to scramble out before she finally sank from view again. Mr Barton kept us informed as soon as he got the details over the wireless.

'D'ye hear there! The Italian submarine *Cobalto* has been rammed and sunk by HMS *Ithuriel*. She is now safely on the bottom where she can do us no harm. *Ithuriel*'s bows are damaged and, with the Italian prisoners aboard, she is proceeding to Gibraltar for repairs.'

It seemed that we weren't doing too badly after all. The convoy had lost one ship, but the enemy had paid a heavy price for it. I began to feel a bit more cheerful. Maybe we did have a chance after all. It had been a broiling hot day, made hotter by the sun's heat reflecting off the deck. Sweat soaked my uniform and ran down my arms and face, trickling through the grime of expended cordite.

'Phew! You could fry an egg on those plates!' said Ron, then regarded me with a critical eye. 'You're dead scruffy, d'you know that?'

'You should see yourself!' I laughed. 'I think I'll ask the ammunition party for a bucket. We can lower it over the side and cool ourselves down. Come to think of it, we can keep the gun cool with it, too.'

'You what? Throw salt water over one of Jack Holder's precious guns – he'll go berserk!'

We both laughed. Holder liked his guns kept spotlessly clean, dry and lightly oiled.

The idea of salt water getting into the working parts would make him do a war dance.

Just over an hour after we'd sunk the submarine the alarm klaxon sounded again. It looked like another big raid, but this time it was coming in from the east.

'Here we go again!' I said, as Bill clipped on a full magazine.

I guessed that we were now out of range of Sardinia and that the raiders were coming from Sicily. Two squadrons of torpedo-bombers came in from different directions with their *motobombas*. Most of them dropped short but one of their torpedoes blew the stern off a destroyer, the *Foresight*, and she was clearly sinking.

At the same time, Stuka dive-bombers attacked from ahead and astern, deliberately splitting our fire. They picked the carrier *Indomitable* as their target. For minutes at a time she vanished from view behind a curtain of water thrown up by near misses. When the curtain parted I could see that there were fires raging on her flight deck, from which blazing petrol was pouring in a fiery waterfall into the sea. Then she turned away downwind to bring her fires under control.

The raid seemed to last for ever. I fought against tiredness and my aching muscles, firing at one target after another until the barrel of the gun was glowing red. We must have become someone's target because we had a near miss right alongside. Bill, Ron and I almost collapsed under the weight of falling water. The gun hissed and sizzled, giving off huge clouds of steam. Then the raiders were gone.

Our unexpected bath had freshened us up.

'Looks like the guns got their shower after all!' Ron said.

We both staggered about, laughing and pointing at the steaming Oerlikon like a pair of lunatics. After all the tension, it was such a relief to laugh.

'Next time it overheats we might just as well lower it over the side!' I said.

'Oh, good grief!' said Ron, shaking with laughter. 'What's Jack going to say about that?'

'Having a good time, lads?'

It was Joey, a youngster from our ammunition party.

'Do us a favour, Joey, and get us a bucket and line, will you?' said Ron, getting himself under control. The surrounding deck was covered in thousands of expended brass cartridge cases, so many that you couldn't move without crunching on them.

'And bring us some brooms, will you, boys? We'll have to clean this mess up if we're to work properly.'

The ammunition party began sweeping the empty cases into the scuppers and over the side. Bill and I were trying to inject some oil into the gun's moving parts when the Tannoy crackled again.

'D'ye hear there! During the last raid our fighters shot down seven enemy aircraft and the ships accounted for a further two. You'll be pleased to hear that *Indomitable* has got her fires under control . . .'

There was a pause. When Mr Barton spoke again his tone was deadly serious.

'We are now approaching the narrows between Sicily and Tunisia. The area contains shallows and known minefields. We shall be using the Skerki Channel and passing close to Cape Bon. There is very little sea room for the battleships and carriers, and as they cannot be risked they and their escort will be turning back very shortly. That was always part of the original plan . . .'

He paused again. You could have heard a pin drop anywhere in the ship.

'As intended, we shall pass through the channel under cover of darkness with the close escort. In the morning, we shall be within range of Malta's fighters. Gun crews and ammunition parties will remain closed up throughout the passage. Good luck. That is all.'

The loudspeakers went dead. No one spoke. There was nothing to say.

I went to the rail and watched *Nelson*, *Rodney*, *Indomitable* and *Victorious* turn away towards the setting sun with their cruisers and destroyers. So far, we'd fought off the enemy's air and submarine attacks with their help, but suddenly they were gone. Now, in addition, we'd have to contend with enemy torpedo boats and, for all we knew, the Italian surface fleet was on its way to intercept us. I had been frightened during the last couple of days, just like everyone else must have been, but for the next few minutes I was gripped by sheer icy terror. I felt it clutch my stomach, run down my back like sweat and shoot through my veins. I felt myself beginning to shake. I swallowed hard and slowly pulled myself together.

'Char.' Bill handed me a mug. I hadn't even seen the cooks coming round. 'And a sausage butty with brown sauce. Don't say I never give you anything.'

We squatted down beside the rail. Bill was a few years older than me, but I'd known him a long time and his folks lived just a few streets away from mine. He knew what was bothering me all right, because I think it was bothering him too.

'Ever bet on the Grand National?' he asked.

I shook my head.

'If you do, stay away from the favourite – it's usually an outsider that wins. That's what we've got – an outside chance, but it's still a chance. And because we're outsiders, we're going to surprise a lot of people.'

I began to see what he was driving at.

'Remember those two Italian pilots pretending to land on the *Victorious*? They got away with it, didn't they? You never know what you can do until you try, do you?'

Bill was a wise old bird and I was glad to be in his company. He'd made me feel better, but I couldn't help thinking that the fate of the entire operation would be decided during the next few hours, and at the back of my mind was the worry about how Mam and Dad would take it if anything happened to Dick or me. Bill was right, though. Thoughts like that don't help in times of danger. I shook them off and walked to the rail.

Chapter 8
Fire Below!

If I had been on a cruise I'd have said it
was a perfect evening. Far behind our stern
the sun was setting in a red glow that
illuminated a flat, calm sea. The heat of the
day had gone and the ship's progress
through the water created a cooling breeze. It
couldn't have been more peaceful.

I watched the convoy merge from four
columns to two as we entered the Skerki
Channel. It was neatly done, with one cruiser,
the *Nigeria*, leading the port column, and
another, the *Cairo*, leading the star-board.
With the rest of the escort gathered round,
the scene was one of quiet, ordered efficiency.

In just a few seconds it was all totally
transformed. There was a tremendous
explosion against the *Ohio*'s port side. I was
flung over backwards, cracking my head

against something. I may have passed out for a while, because the next thing I saw were flames leaping skywards, figures running and shouts of 'Fire below!'

I staggered to my feet. A second was all it took for me to take in the living nightmare. *Cairo*'s stern had been blown off and she was sinking. Even as I watched, another torpedo hit *Nigeria* amidships. All order dissolved before my eyes as ships took evasive action to avoid running into the stricken warships and each other.

I shook my head to clear it. *Ohio*'s damage was all too apparent. A huge hole had been blown in her port side amidships. The blast had also punched a smaller hole in the starboard side and left a great tear in the deck. Water was flooding into the damaged tank. Kerosene from adjoining tanks had begun to blaze, the flames roaring through the buckled plates.

When there's a fire aboard a tanker, everyone joins in putting it out, no matter what their rank. Captain Mason was in the thick of it, directing jets for the deck water lines and shouting for more extinguishers amid the searing heat. I ran to join Ron, Bill and the rest of the gun crews to give a hand.

But Mason waved us away. 'Back to your guns, lads!' he shouted. 'There's another air attack coming in! Leave this to us – it's what we're all trained for!'

As I reached the gun I saw the enemy planes drone in, Ju-88s and Savoia torpedo-bombers, wave after wave of them. They dropped bombs, torpedoes and parachute mines. We kept firing incessantly, but now the barrage was only a shadow of what it had once been. With a blaze raging amidships, we were an obvious target. Water from near misses cascaded regularly on to the decks.

'Just give it what you can, lads,' Bill shouted above the noise.

It was a scene of utter confusion as ships tried to avoid one another and torpedoes at the same time. There was a lot of shouting from the Bofors crew. Some seamen ran aft, carrying fenders. I could see that the *Empire Hope*, immediately astern, was bearing down on us. There were men on her forecastle, too, dropping fenders over the bows, but in a minute or two she would slice right into our stern. I heard her skipper ring down for Hard Astern. She put her wheel over and a collision was avoided by a whisker.

At the height of the action, as dusk was

gathering, one of the American ships, the *Almeria Lykes*, came past. To my horror, I saw that a parachute had snagged on the bridge wing and below it a mine dangled, swinging gently to and fro. Knowing what the mine could do if one of its horns touched the hull, I held my breath. A man appeared, opened a clasp knife and began cutting through the parachute lines.

'If he's not careful he'll get his tin hat blown off!' said Ron.

'Chances are his head will be in it!' I replied.

The man continued to cut away until the mine dropped harmlessly into the sea and drifted astern. He gave us a wave and disappeared from view.

'She's got a great bunch aboard her,' I remarked to Bill. 'I met some of them when you sent me on that shore job back at Greenock. They just don't seem bothered by all this uproar.'

'You're right,' said Bill. 'This is their first convoy, too, isn't it?'

'Yes, but they're pretty relaxed about it. One of them said to me, "You guys have been doing this for years – just show us how it's done and we'll not let you down!" '

'They're not, either,' said Bill.

Bill was right. I felt ashamed of my earlier doubts about the Merchant Navy.

We had now stopped and the convoy pulled steadily away from us. In the space of just a few minutes we had lost three more ships. The *Brisbane Star* was hit in the bows by a torpedo. Out of control, she swerved wildly towards the *Empire Hope*, which stopped her engines to avoid being rammed. Dive-bombers immediately pounced on the stationary target. She was hit and quickly became an inferno when her cased petrol went up. We could see her boats pulling away through a spreading lake of blazing fuel.

Shortly after, the *Clan Ferguson* was hit several times. During the next few minutes she simply blew herself apart in a huge pillar of flame and smoke as her cargo of ammunition exploded. For hundreds of yards around, the sea was covered by more burning petrol.

Then something amazing happened.

'Submarine two miles on the port bow!' shouted the bridge look-out.

Captain Mason ran across from the fire and peered through his powerful night binoculars.

'Shall I man the five-inch, sir?' asked Bill.

'No,' said Mason. 'Take a look at what she's doing.'

Bill took a look and then silently handed me the binoculars. We had been trained to recognize British and German submarines. This was neither, so she must have been Italian. Her crew were busy on deck, hauling the *Clan Ferguson*'s survivors out of the blazing sea.

'That man is a gentleman,' said Mason quietly. 'We can all respect an enemy like that.'

Soon we had our own fires under control. Shortly afterwards, the destroyer *Ashanti* came alongside.

'*Ohio*, ahoy!'

It was Rear-Admiral Burrough, commander of the close escort, who had evidently transferred his flag to the destroyer when *Nigeria* was so badly hit. Captain Mason went to the rail.

'Are you all right?' the admiral hailed.

'Fine, thanks,' shouted Mason. 'We can attend to this.'

The admiral told Mason he was dispatching the crippled *Nigeria* to Gibraltar, escorted by three destroyers, but that Vice-

Admiral Syfret, who commanded the battleships and carriers, was sending back one of his own cruisers and two destroyers to make up our numbers.

'I've got to go on with the rest of the convoy,' Burrough shouted. 'Take the shore route if you can and slip across to Malta. They need you badly.'

'Don't worry, sir, we'll do our best,' called Mason.

Then the *Ashanti* was gone, leaving us alone in the gathering darkness, save for the *Brisbane Star* in the distance, also stopped. Near her, the lakes of petrol continued to burn. The *Ohio*'s officers and crew worked flat out to repair the worst of the damage. I heard from various parts of the ship the sounds of hammering and banging.

'Must be shoring up the bulkheads below,' I commented.

Bruce Cameron appeared. He was sweating heavily. His face, arms and white uniform all seemed to be covered with a greasy grey film. He slumped over the rail, sucking in great gulps of air.

'You OK there, mate?' I asked.

It took him a minute or two to reply.

'Feeling a bit crook, that's all. Must have

sucked in too much smoke and kerosene fumes. I'll be fine.'

'How's the ship, sir?' asked Bill.

Bruce's twisted grin appeared, so he must have been feeling better.

'There's bad news and good news,' he said. 'I'll give you the bad news first. The hole and the flooded tank you know about. The gyro compass is smashed and the blast has shifted the magnetic compass off its mounting. The steering's gone and the engine-room burners have been blown out. The good news is that it's a fine starry night so we can use dead reckoning. We can steer by operating the valve on the steering engine on the poop. Mr Gray and Mr Stephen will be looking after that. Of course, they can't see where they're going, so the skipper will tell them what he wants by telephone from the bridge. There's more good news: the electricity will be back on in five minutes and the chief reckons he'll have the engines started in half an hour.'

He paused to wipe the sweat from the inside of his cap with a grubby handkerchief, frowning as he did so.

'There you are,' said Bill, turning to me. 'Didn't I tell you we were in with a chance?'

'Trouble is,' said Bruce thoughtfully, 'we'll have to take it easy until we see how she stands up to it. We don't want her breaking her back.'

If the ship broke into two halves it was probable that both would sink. Suddenly, I didn't need Bill to keep my spirits up. Our situation was really worse than it had ever been but I wasn't scared any more. All at once, I started to see the funny side of things.

'You know what?' I said. 'When I told people I was going to sea they said it was good for the character – it'll make a man out of you, they said!'

We all roared with laughter.

'Betcha the blokes who told you that are all tucked up, snug in bed ashore!' said Bruce. He wandered off, still chuckling.

The word was, the skipper had taken a fix on the stars and decided to follow the admiral's advice by steering close to the Tunisian coast. At 20.45 the engines rumbled into life. We began moving slowly while the ship's officers carefully examined the cracks in the hull. When they found they weren't getting any worse, the speed was steadily increased until we were proceeding as normally as possible, given that we steered in a series of curves rather than a straight line.

It was the sort of dark-blue velvet night you get in the Mediterranean, with the sea and sky blending together. A destroyer, emerging from the darkness, pulled alongside out of nowhere. She was the *Ledbury*. I heard Captain Mason explaining our navigational problems and then saw she had rigged a shaded blue light on her stern so we could follow her.

There was no sign of the *Brisbane Star*, so she must have got herself moving again, too. There were, however, still pools of blazing petrol marking the spots where *the Empire Hope* and the *Clan Ferguson* had gone down, and *Ledbury* seemed to be heading for one of them. The skipper rushed out on to the bridge wing with his loud-hailer.

'For God's sake keep clear of that!' he shouted. 'We're leaking kerosene!'

Both ships executed an emergency turn away from the danger.

A flashing light appeared in the distance to starboard. It was the lighthouse on Cape Bon. It passed abeam, then slid astern. For the moment, everything was peaceful, so the skipper decided to hold a roll-call. Two of our blokes, Hands and another Smith, were missing, and so was a galley boy. The ship's No. 5 lifeboat was found trailing from the falls and Ron remembered that when the fire broke out he'd seen them trying to get it ready for launching. I suppose they thought they were making themselves useful. Unfortunately, they weren't used to handling the machinery and it looked very much as though they'd been thrown out into the sea. Another man, a steward who'd been with an ammunition party, had been washed overboard by the deluge from one of the near misses. We resigned ourselves to the fact that they were all lost overboard. A mood of gloom descended on us.

From time to time the horizon ahead flickered with gunfire and explosions, and sometimes we saw lines of tracer flashing across the surface of the sea.

'What's going on?' I asked.

'I'm not sure,' said Bill. 'We're close to Pantelleria, an island halfway between Sicily and Tunisia. The Italians base torpedo boats there, so maybe they've sent them out after the convoy.'

We did not see any torpedo boats ourselves

and had no idea what was happening to the rest of the convoy.

As dawn approached, however, we started to pass by the now-familiar lakes of blazing petrol and areas of charred wreckage. I began to wonder what terrible thing we might find ahead. We were now travelling at something like our normal speed. Ominously, the vibration was causing the jagged steel edges of the crack across the deck to grind together. It was a horrible noise, like someone dragging a shovel along a wall, and it set our teeth on edge. Would the *Ohio* be able to hold out?

Chapter 9
Unexploded Bomb

At last the long night ended. I'd no idea how hungry I was until the cooks came round; fortunately, there was plenty for everyone. As the light strengthened we became aware that the enemy's shadowing aircraft were back, so it was no surprise when the alarm klaxon signalled an incoming air attack.

I saw six twin-engined aircraft come into view, flying high and fast. We opened up with everything we'd got.

'Cease firing!' shouted Bill unexpectedly. He and Jack Holder began running round the gun positions.

'Cease firing! Cease firing! They're Beaufighters from Malta!'

By now we were so tired and so used to being attacked that we treated every aircraft as an enemy. It was a comfort to know that we had reached the edge of the air cover Malta could provide, even though we weren't within range of her Spitfires yet. Fortunately, we didn't seem to have done any damage and the Beaufighters chased off the enemy's shadowing aircraft.

Shortly after, we caught up the convoy – what there was left of it. There were just two cruisers, the *Kenya*, with her damaged bows, and the *Charybdis*, which had been sent up to join us during the night, and seven destroyers; of the merchant vessels, only *Port Chalmers*, *Melbourne Star*, *Waimarama*, *Rochester Castle* and *Dorset* were left. Small wonder, then, we got a warm welcome when we appeared, or that everyone cheered when we got a wireless message from the *Brisbane Star* that she was miles astern but following on at 13 knots.

We were not given long to celebrate rejoining the convoy. The Beaufighters, flying at their extreme operational range, could not give us permanent cover. At 08.00 the first air attack of the day came in, delivered by a dozen Ju-88s. Ignoring the exploding flak and lines of tracer, they came diving down from about 6,000 feet. I saw the *Waimarama*, next but one ahead of us, straddled by bursting bombs and hit several times. Fierce fires erupted fore and aft, then she suddenly blew up in a huge eruption of flame and smoke. The *Melbourne Star*, immediately behind her, took violent evasive action, and so did we. Even so, we were both hit by a rain of flying metal fragments and burning debris. The kerosene bubbling through the buckled deck caught fire again, but the fire-fighting parties went into action immediately and quickly got the blaze under control. It angered me to see the *Waimarama* get so far and then be blown to pieces.

Meanwhile, we kept firing away until the gun developed a serious jam. A cartridge case had split in the breech so that it couldn't be extracted, which in turn meant that no further rounds could be loaded.

'My tool box is in the five-inch locker. Go get it now!' shouted Bill.

I raced off to fetch it. While I was rummaging I glanced up at the Bofors mounting. The gun crew were working together like the well-drilled team they were, the layers cranking their traverse and elevation handles constantly to keep the enemy in their ring sights, and the loaders pushing in the steady stream of four-round clips that 'Hangman' Collins was bringing up on his hoist.

Back at the gun, it took us a while to prise the offending brass cylinder out of the Oerlikon's breech. By then, the next raid was coming in and we were at it hammer and tongs again. This time it was Stukas, which were making the *Ohio* their special target. I could see their bombs as soon as they released them. They seemed to be heading straight at you, then you'd be drenched by a near miss. As they pulled out of their dive, the Stukas' rear-gunners gave the ship a long burst each.

There were bullets cracking and whining all over the place. Normally, you'd dive for cover, but as nowhere seemed safer than anywhere else, we just kept firing back. Anyway, it did us good to see our rounds going into those ugly black fuselages and stitching their crooked wings. It was the blokes down below in the engine room I felt sorry for. All they could do was listen to the racket going on and hope that the next one didn't bring the sea pouring in through the side.

Suddenly, there was an explosion towards the foredeck. The ship shuddered and I saw a mass of water cascading down on to the deck. Above all the noise I could hear the howl of a dive-bomber's engine. It seemed to be getting louder and louder.

'Look out!' shouted someone.

I spun round and saw the Stuka bearing down on us. The starboard Oerlikons, the Brownings and the Bofors had engaged the plane but it continued towards us, regardless of the fire coming at it. It was a battle of wills: he wasn't giving up, and neither were we. The aircraft was now dangerously close but still it came down without a hint that it would pull out of its dive.

'Get down!' shouted Bill. 'He's going to crash aboard!'

We flung ourselves to the deck. It shook violently as the Stuka smashed on to our foredeck. As the smoke cleared I could see a wing was resting against the bridge, like a dead bird. Inside the shattered canopy were the goggled figures of the pilot and his rear-gunner, both of them obviously dead. Petrol gushed over the deck from the plane's ruptured tanks. The fire fighters sprang into action at once, using the deck water lines to swill it over the side.

'That was a lucky escape,' exclaimed Ron.

We approached the wreckage cautiously.

'Watch out!' shouted a voice. 'It's still got a bomb attached!' Everyone stopped dead in their tracks. Maybe we hadn't been so lucky.

Jack Holder appeared with his armourer's kit. He was probably the only man aboard who could handle the situation.

'Right, I need two volunteers now!' he said.

Everyone looked around, shuffling their feet nervously.

'I'll have a go,' said Bill stepping forward.

Jack shook his head.

'Not you, chum. You're the only other armourer aboard and there's no way we can both take the risk. Come on, someone else,' he barked.

'Count me in.'

I heard myself speak before I realized what I was doing.

'And me,' said another voice. It was Ron.

As I crawled into the cramped space under the smashed fuselage I thought of what Captain Mason had said about being called upon to do extra duties. I had to do this for Dick and for the sake of the mission. Jack examined the bomb as carefully as a doctor examines his patient.

'Thousand-pounder,' he said. 'Pilot must have been killed before he could release it. Get us some flour sacks from the galley, will you? It's not armed, but I don't want it dropping on the deck when we release the clamps.'

Ron wriggled out and rounded up a party which returned with a dozen sacks of flour. Jack built them up into a pile below the bomb. Beneath the fuselage it was hot, sweaty and stank of petrol.

'How do you know it's not armed?' I whispered.

Jack pointed to a small propeller.

'See this? When the bomb's released it starts spinning as it passes through the air. It moves a rod which exposes the detonator. It's a safety device that prevents the bomb exploding while it's being handled. All very simple and neat. If you look you can see the propeller hasn't moved.'

'Does that mean the bomb is safe?' I asked hopefully.

'No, you can't take anything for granted in this game. For all we know, the crash may have exposed the detonator anyway. Still glad you volunteered?'

I was beginning to feel very uneasy. It's

one thing to be blazing away with an Oerlikon when you're driven by anger, but this was different. It required ice-cold courage.

'I wouldn't do your job for twice the money,' I said.

'And I don't fancy yours much! Now, you two support the tail fins while I loosen the rear-end clamps,' he said, chuckling. 'When the clamps open, let the tail down gently.'

He worked away with various tools until the jaws opened. The immense weight came as a surprise, but we did as he told us.

'Now for the difficult part,' he said. 'Move round and support the nose while I deal with the forward clamp. It will be much heavier but it hasn't so far to fall. If you're fond of your fingers, keep them out of harm's way.'

Although we were supporting it, the bomb dropped with a heavy thump and I tensed, expecting the worst. Nothing happened. Jack wiped the sweat off his forehead.

'That's a bit of luck,' he said. 'The fuse is on top. I'll just strip it out.'

'What if it's booby-trapped?' asked Ron. There had been plenty of examples of this during the blitz. My mouth went dry as Jack began unscrewing the cap.

'Unlikely,' he said as the fuse started to emerge. 'That's all very well if you're dropping delayed-action bombs on land. At sea, it's mostly a waste of time.'

It was the word 'mostly' that worried me.

'There, that's that,' he said at length, holding up the disconnected fuse.

Ron and I both sighed with relief.

'Now, we'll rearrange the sacks into a slope and roll the bomb very slowly out into the open.'

When we emerged from under the wreckage there was a crowd watching us from what they thought was a safe distance.

'Mr Cameron, sir!' shouted Jack. 'I want six strong lads to heave this thing over the side! These two have done their bit.'

Ron and I walked slowly over to Bill.

'Well done,' he said quietly, patting us both on the back. We didn't say anything, because after all he'd volunteered for the job himself. We watched the bomb being carried gingerly to the rail and thrown overboard. There was a great cheer as it plunged into the water.

Chapter 10
Abandon Ship!

A few hours after the bomb incident, I had finally relaxed and was able to feel quietly proud of the part I'd played. The enemy never left us alone for too long though and the alarm sounded.

'Action Stations!'

After we'd repelled the initial attack, a second wave came in, twenty strong, dropping parachute mines, circling torpedoes and bombs. We immediately made an emergency turn but two sticks of bombs landed on either side of the ship.

Kaboosh!

I actually felt the *Ohio* lift out of the water. She dropped back with a tremendous crash that threw everyone off their feet. Tons of water crashed down on the deck, but amazingly the ship kept going as her propeller bit into the water again.

Dazed, I scrambled up and returned to the gun. We were near-missed again on the starboard side, close to the engine room. The lack of vibration beneath our feet told me that the engines had stopped. The *Ohio* was slowing and, once again, the convoy was pulling away from us.

Twenty agonizing minutes later, the engineers somehow got us on the move again. *Ohio* surged forward, her speed rising steadily until she was doing close to 15 knots. I felt an enormous sense of relief. Most of the attacking planes had left apart from one Junkers, which made a final pass. At that point a stick of bombs crashed just alongside. The engines shuddered into silence again. We slowed to a standstill, wallowing slowly in a gentle swell. Although two destroyers, the *Ledbury* and the *Penn*, were standing by, the convoy had all but disappeared. As the minutes ticked away I began to understand what a sitting duck feels like in broad daylight.

I shouted to Bruce Cameron. 'What's happening?'

His expression was deadly serious.

'It's bad,' he said. 'The blast has smashed the electric fuel pumps. The chief and the second engineer are crawling around the bilges trying to connect the steam pumps before the boiler pressure drops too low.'

I tried to picture the two men working amid the oily slime of the narrow space between the engine-room floor plates and the ship's keel, with only their torches to penetrate the inky darkness. A horrible thought struck me.

'But if a bomb or torpedo hits that part of the ship . . .'

'Don't even think about it,' said Bruce. 'But yeah, you're right, they'd be drowned like rats in a trap as soon as the engine room started to flood.'

Noon came and went. Eventually there was a rumble as the engines were started again. We all cheered as *Ohio* began to move slowly, but something was obviously badly wrong. The smoke emerging from the funnel was no longer a steady black stream, but black mingled with white. After a few minutes the engines sputtered and died again. The engine-room staff, whom we called the Black Gang because they were usually grubby with oil and grease, started coming out on deck.

'Sorry, lads,' said one of them, 'water has got into the fuel. There's nothing we can do about it until the boilers cool down.'

They were a great bunch, the Black Gang. Some of them wanted to give us a hand at the guns, but once they saw what an air attack looked like they decided they'd been better off not knowing and disappeared below again. You can't blame them for that. The cooks were another good bunch. Mealtimes were just a memory now, but they were always on the go, bringing round tea, coffee and sandwiches no matter what was going on. They said keeping busy was better than sitting around as it kept their minds occupied.

Ledbury had been sent off on another job, but *Penn* came alongside. Her skipper, a Lieutenant-Commander Swain, hailed Captain Mason.

'I'm going to try and tow you out of this, Captain. Can you take a ten-inch manila rope?'

'Yes, we can,' shouted Mason. 'We'll need to do a bit of tidying up first, though.'

He dispatched Second Officer McKilligan with a party of seamen to the foredeck, where they began pitching the wreckage of the crashed Stuka overboard. Then the heavy 10-inch manila rope was dragged over and secured with four turns around the bollards.

Penn began moving slowly ahead. The rope straightened and groaned as it tightened its grip. It was a sight I had watched many times at the Pier Head in Liverpool as ferries moored bows-on against the fast Mersey tide, and I had often wondered how the ropes stood up to the terrific strain. *Penn*, her screws churning the water into foam, came to a standstill as she took *Ohio*'s immense weight, then began forging very slowly ahead.

We followed, but, as the huge hole in our side began acting as a rudder, we swung steadily to port until we were at 90 degrees to the destroyer. Without power for our steering engine, there was nothing we could do to help. Strangely, when *Penn* stopped pulling, the *Ohio*'s bows straightened until once more she was pointing in the direction of Malta, as though telling us which way she wanted to go. *Penn* tried again, with the same result.

'It won't work!' shouted Mason. 'The only way is either to tow from alongside or with two ships, one ahead and the other astern.' Unfortunately, at that moment there wasn't another ship to help. To make matters worse, a heavier air attack than usual was coming in. To prevent us both being sitting ducks, *Penn* went full ahead to snap the tow, the end coiling back on to our foredeck like a striking snake. Guns barking, she began to circle us like a protective sheepdog. After that, I was too busy to notice much else as I engaged one target after another.

'Look out!' shouted Bill, pointing upwards.

Once again, a Stuka was diving directly down on the ship. All the *Ohio*'s guns focused on him at once. He flew straight into a concentrated cone of fire. Bits started to fly off the aircraft. I saw him release a bomb, then he blew up. The bomb entered the water to explode beneath us, in just the same area that the torpedo had struck our side. I felt the ship heave a little.

As the raiders left, Captain Mason and Lieutenant Barton came running along the deck to inspect the damage. The crack had widened and the sea was now flowing into another of the tanks. Mason's expression was grim.

'I think that one broke her back,' he said.

He hailed *Penn* to tell her what had happened.

'There's nothing more we can do at the moment,' Swain shouted. 'We'll have to wait for dark. You're just risking your lives for no purpose, so why don't you abandon ship for the present and come aboard here? You can go back tonight.'

'I don't think she's going to last that long,' Mason replied. 'Thanks, we will come aboard if you don't mind.'

I felt terribly weary. How many days and nights had we been at it now? I couldn't remember. It wasn't just the lack of sleep, or the fact that my feet ached and my ankles were swollen from hours of standing. My mind was completely drained by the reaction to being in constant danger and the terrible disappointment that, having brought her so far, we were having to abandon the *Ohio*.

'How far are we from Malta, sir?' I asked Mr Barton.

'About seventy miles at the last reckoning.'

'I thought we were going to have some air cover,' I said. I wasn't bitter, just terribly frustrated. 'The other side have been having it pretty much all their own way.'

'I know what you mean,' he said quietly, 'but we're not quite within effective range of the Spitfires yet. Just the same, they've not been idle. The last I heard before the wireless went off was that the enemy has been flying at sea level when he leaves Sicily to prevent being picked up on Malta's radar, and he's only climbing to attack height when he's closing in. Once we got on to his little game the RAF started breaking up his attacks south of Sicily – otherwise things here would be much worse than they are.'

I looked around *Ohio*'s torn deck, her fire-blackened paintwork and her superstructure scarred everywhere by bomb splinters and machine-gun bullets. It was hard to see how things could be much worse.

'That a fact, sir?'

We both chuckled.

'You'd better get along,' he said.

The ship's officers rounded everyone up. *Penn* came alongside, her fenders out. There was just a foot or two of water between our two hulls. I jumped out and down. Hands grabbed me, hauling me over the rail. The destroyer was already crowded with survivors from other ships, but they made room willingly enough. Bill and I flopped down in an empty corner and then sleep overwhelmed me.

Chapter 11
All Hands!

Old sailors will tell you that ships are alive and have a mind of their own. They'll tell you about unlucky ships on which men die in accidents that have no apparent cause, and lucky ships that survive terrible ordeals against all the odds. A few will even tell you that they've served aboard ships that were haunted. *Ohio* was either very lucky or very unlucky – it depended on how you looked at it. But no one could deny that she had spirit.

Four hours after we'd abandoned her I was still fathoms down in a deep sleep. I seemed to hear a voice calling.

'*Ohio*, all hands! Wakey, wakey!'

Someone was shaking me.

'Come on, rise and shine! We're going back aboard!' Ron said cheerfully.

With a real effort, I surfaced. I looked at

my watch. It said a quarter-to-six and it took me a little while to work out that it was evening. I hadn't expected to see the *Ohio* again, but there she was, battered but still afloat.

Evidently she had taken on quite a lot of water because now there was only 3 or 4 feet between the sea and her deck. Near by was a minesweeper, the *Rye*, and two armed launches, Nos. 121 and 168, which someone told me had come out from Malta to meet us. As the *Penn* carefully came alongside I found myself standing next to Bruce Cameron.

'I'm surprised she hasn't gone down by now,' I said.

'They say tankers die hard,' he replied. 'They're divided into so many compartments that if a few of them get flooded the rest will hold her up. Just the same, seeing the state she's in, I'm pretty surprised, too.'

Captain Mason led us back aboard. The deck crew began getting us ready for towing again, the engineers disappeared below to rig the manual steering, and we DEMS gunners went back to our guns. Already they were coated with rust and dried salt. We set to, cleaning off the worst of it with oily rags, and easing the moving parts with oil.

Jack Holder, the naval gunnery instructor and armourer, arrived.

'Don't blame me if we get multiple stoppages, chum,' said Bill. 'Just look at it!'

Holder nodded. It must have broken his heart to see his beautifully maintained guns in this condition.

'Can't be helped,' he said. 'Everyone's in the same boat. Any spare barrels left?'

'We've used the lot,' answered Bill. 'They're all shot out now – rounds are going all over the place.'

'At this rate we'll end up throwing rocks at 'em!' said Holder grimly.

We started to move again, very slowly. *Penn* was towing from ahead and our rudder was set to starboard to balance the drag of the hole in the ship's port side. There was still a tendency to swing in that direction but this was countered when *Rye* passed a line which we made fast amidships on the starboard side. Soon we were making a steady 4 or 5 knots. The worst of our troubles seemed over.

At 18.30 we picked up the familiar sound of German engines. I could see four Ju-88s coming in low from astern. As we let fly at them I could hear Captain Mason shouting for the engine-room staff to come up. One bomb landed just astern, jamming the rudder immovably.

Kaboom!

Another smashed through the boat deck. There was an explosion deep inside the ship. The engineers, who had been sheltering in a companionway, came staggering out on deck, half-blind, choking and covered in blue asbestos dust.

'What's happened?' I shouted.

'That last one must have gone through two decks and hit a boiler!' spluttered one of them, beating the dust off himself. 'Lucky for us it was cold! Even so, there won't be much left of the engine room. This muck is lagging. It's been blown everywhere and you just can't breathe below deck.'

The explosion from below reached upwards, unseating one of the engine-room ventilators. I shouted as I saw it topple on to the Bofors mounting, but it was too late.

'For God's sake give us a hand!' shouted Bombardier Labarn. 'We've got a man trapped under here!'

There was a rush of feet as men ran aft. Bill left me to handle the gun and he and Ron

113

ran to join them. They returned a few minutes later.

'It's Gunner Brown,' Bill said. 'They've got him out but he's in a bad way.'

The tow had been cast off as *Penn* and *Rye* joined in the battle for survival. The three of us were putting up a concentrated barrage in a small area, so that although more waves of attacking aircraft appeared, they shied away and the worst we got was another soaking from a near miss that dropped beside the foredeck. After the raiders had gone I looked round and saw Captain Mason examining the rent in the deck with Mr Wyld, the chief engineer. The great rip in the plating now not only stretched further across the deck, but it was also much wider.

'So far as I can tell, it's only the keel plate that's holding her together,' said Wyld. 'She's also shipping water aft – the engine room has started to flood.'

'That's it, then,' replied Mason heavily. 'Unless we get more ships to help with the tow she doesn't stand a chance. We'd better get everyone off again.'

The two launches had been expecting this and were standing by. Mr Wyld, Mr Gray and about half the lads clambered aboard 168. She cast off and that was the last we saw of them for a while. No. 121 came alongside. Brown was lifted gently across the gap and then the rest of us piled aboard. Captain Mason appeared at the *Ohio*'s rail, carrying a brief-case containing the ship's papers. He looked sad and thoughtful.

'I think I'll stay with her,' he said quietly.

'Don't be an idiot!' shouted the lieutenant commanding the launch. 'You can't do anything more for her and she could go under any minute!'

None of *Ohio*'s crew liked a stranger talking to their skipper like that, but we also knew the officer was right. I couldn't help myself shouting out.

'He's got a point, sir. Toss us your bag!'

Mason hesitated for a moment, looking at our pleading faces, then did so, jumping after it. I was relieved he had chosen to come with us. It would have been a waste to lose such a great man.

The launch took us across to *Penn*, where Brown was carried to the sick bay immediately.

'Get some rest, lads,' said a petty officer.

He nodded in the direction of the wallowing *Ohio*. 'We'll do what we can to save her.'

The sun was setting. My thoughts at that moment were gloomy. *Ohio* had put up a terrific fight and, even if she had finally lost, she had nothing to be ashamed of. I didn't expect to see her again.

Chapter 12
The Longest Miles

It was the grey light of dawn when Bill shook me awake. His expression was serious as he signalled me to follow him. We made our way aft to where the *Ohio*'s hands were gathered. Brown had died from his injuries shortly after being brought aboard the *Penn*. His body, wrapped in canvas, was lying on a grating under a White Ensign. Captain Mason read the familiar and comforting words from *The Book of Common Prayer*. At the appropriate point, the bos'n tipped the grating and the body slipped over the side.

After a moment's silence Commander Swain appeared beside the skipper. We were glad that he had taken the trouble to join us.

'I thought we could all do with some good news,' he said. 'Yesterday evening, the *Port Chalmers*, *Rochester Castle* and *Melbourne*

Star all reached Valletta safely. Needless to say, they got a terrific welcome.'

At least some good had come from all our efforts.

'How about *Dorset*?' asked Captain Mason.

Swain shook his head. 'I'm afraid she didn't get there.' He pointed to another destroyer lying near by. '*Bramham* picked up her survivors and came straight on to help us. *Ledbury* has also rejoined, so there's enough of us now to have another shot at towing.'

'In that case,' said Mason, 'as *Ohio* is our ship we'd be glad if you'd put us back aboard her. The trouble is, we're going to be short-handed, so we'd be grateful for any help you can let us have.'

'I've more than enough survivors aboard,' replied Swain. 'Plenty of them will be happy to make your numbers up, and I can detail a few of our ratings as well.'

I suppose in a way the crowd who boarded *Ohio* that morning represented the whole convoy. Apart from us, the original members of the crew, there were seamen who had survived the loss of their own ships, British and American, a few DEMS gunners from other ships and the ratings *Penn* sent over.

The first thing we found was that whoever had been aboard during the night had done a good job of looting the ship. The canteen had been stripped bare and everything else of value had gone. I suppose they thought it was all on its way to the bottom, anyway. Two of the Oerlikons had disappeared, probably to replace *Penn*'s worn-out guns, which shows the terrible condition they must have been in. Even the ring sights on the remaining Oerlikons had been taken by souvenir hunters.

An hour later we began to make real progress, with *Rye* towing, *Penn* lashed alongside and *Ledbury* holding our stern steady while *Bramham* circled protectively round us with three more minesweepers from Malta, *Speedy*, *Hebe* and *Hythe*. It wasn't plain sailing by any means because, for various reasons, the tow ropes kept snapping and had to be replaced. As *Ohio* sank deeper in the water the order of towing had to be changed, too. We ended up with *Rye* towing from ahead and *Penn* and *Bramham* lashed on either side.

Hour after hour, the tanker's battered hull kept groaning and grating horribly, but when all the rules said she should be on the bottom, she still kept going. Those of us who'd been with her longest imagined she was telling us that she would get us there in the end, but she needed all the help she could get from her friends.

The enemy, of course, was still desperate to sink her. At 10.45 their first air attack came in. Working the guns without sights wasn't easy, but luckily we were used to them now. I focused on one Ju-88 and he went straight into the sea, throttles wide open. The rest of his formation swerved away from the barrage, bombing wildly. A near miss ahead proved to be an oil bomb which sent blazing liquid over the bows, but the fire fighters quickly got the situation under control.

We could see three more German formations closing in and I prepared for the onslaught. This time, however, things were different. Two squadrons of Spitfires came swooping down, breaking up the formations and sending Junkers into their last flaming dive. Yelling with delight, we waved our tin hats as our fighters chased the enemy all over the sky.

Despite their efforts, however, three of the

bombers from the last formation broke through, heading straight for us with a section of Spitfires in hot pursuit. I saw a 1,000-pound bomb leave the belly of a Ju-88. Convinced it would hit, I flung myself to the deck with a yell of 'Get down!'

The bomb sailed over the poop to explode close astern. The blast blew in more plates and increased the rate at which the engine room was flooding. It also pushed the *Ohio* forward so that for a moment the tow to *Rye* went slack. The minesweeper's speed increased because of this, with the result that when the thick manila rope was pulled taut again, it snapped. While that was being sorted out, the launch collected portable pumps from the warships. These slowed down the rate at which the flood in the engine room was rising. I heard someone say we had only 40 miles left to go and again I thought of Dick.

'Nearly there, Dick, nearly there,' I whispered to myself.

The Spitfires were now overhead constantly. When we were not manning the guns we joined the working parties at the ropes. They parted regularly under the strain, or had to be changed to conform with alterations in the towing pattern. It was another broiling-hot day. The constant heavy work of heaving and taking the strain while ropes were shackled and unshackled soon soaked our clothes with sweat and left our hands torn and bleeding. Captain Mason was everywhere, encouraging and setting an example.

I was working in a party under Bruce Cameron. He was pretty good, too. If we were presented with a problem, he thought it through, gave a few quiet orders, and that was that. I remembered how Bill had once told me off for being too familiar with him. He'd told me that, despite being a good bloke and the same age as me, Bruce was still an officer and had a lot of responsibility, so I should respect him and address him properly. Bill was right, of course, and I meant to do something about it, but Bruce was so easygoing it didn't seem to matter.

Later that day, the work party was taking a break, stretched out on the deck, backs against a bulkhead. We were running with sweat, exhausted and, I've got to admit, bad tempered. I was sitting next to a big, surly naval rating called Conlon. I don't know which ship he'd come from but he had the sort of face you wouldn't want to meet on a dark night. We'd just got our breath back when Bruce appeared.

'Come on, fellers,' he said, 'they've got another job for us.'

We clambered wearily to our feet, all except Conlon.

'Get lost!' he said. 'I don't take orders from the Merchant Navy!'

'Worn out, are you?' Bruce snapped back at him. 'Well, we're all worn out, so what's so special about you? If the rest of us can work, so can you! Now, on your feet, you useless drongo!'

I'm certain Conlon would never have dared to take a swing at one of his own officers, but he may have thought he could get away with it this time. I saw his big fists close into balls and the murderous look in his eye as he started to heave himself up.

He would have made two of me, but the way he'd spoken to Bruce had really angered me. While he was still off balance, I shoved my hand in his face and banged his head hard against the bulkhead. Before he could recover from his surprise I pressed my face close to his.

'Listen, you,' I said, 'we've brought this ship a long way through everything they

123

could throw at us! Want to know why? I'll tell you. It's because we had no one but top-rate seamen aboard – *merchant seamen* – the very best! Against them, you just don't count! And while we're on the subject, that's a ship's officer you're talking to!' It was the second time I'd defended the Merchant Navy – but this time I meant every word of it.

'Now, are you going to give us a hand or not?'

Conlon looked round, found he had no support and, like all his type, started to whine.

'I never said I wouldn't do my fair whack!' he complained.

'What's your weight?' Bruce asked him sharply.

'Fourteen stone – sir. Why?'

'Because if I catch you pulling one ounce less than that I swear I'll pitch you over the side!'

'I'll give you a hand, sir!' said Ron.

'So will I!' said someone else.

After that, we had no more trouble from Conlon.

As the afternoon wore on, I saw a dark smudge come up over the horizon. It was Malta! After all we'd been through it was a joy to see her. Gradually it solidified into a coastline. We began to move very slowly along the southern coast. It seemed that we were being shadowed by a submarine, because *Ledbury* began dropping depth-charges every twenty minutes. At Captain Mason's request she stopped because the shock waves were aggravating the damage already sustained by *Ohio*'s battered hull.

Night fell and we ploughed slowly but steadily on. Malta, we knew, bristled with coastal defence batteries. At last I was beginning to feel safe. Suddenly, however, we were brilliantly illuminated by a searchlight ashore, revealing our position to friend and foe alike. Aboard the *Speedy* the signal lamp began to blink angrily, instructing the land crew to turn off the light before we were all blown up. The searchlight snapped off and I relaxed once more.

Later, some miles astern, more search-lights came on and for a while there was the sound of heavy guns firing. Commander Swain called across that the submarine had surfaced and was coming after us at speed when she had been picked up by the shore radar. She had then dived amid a cascade of bursting shells.

Quiet returned, then there was more gunfire. This time many searchlights blazed into life, illuminating a broad corridor across the sea behind us. The enemy, it seemed, just couldn't resist having one last crack at us. They were the same torpedo boats that had done so much damage off Cape Bon but, like the submarine, they must have been picked up on radar. After a short barrage from the coastal defence batteries, they gave up and went home.

We swung north around the eastern end of the island, then entered the cleared channel through our own minefield. Off Zonqor Point we were due to steer north-west for the last few miles to Valletta. Unfortunately, the bend in the channel was too sharp and the channel itself was too narrow for us to proceed in the towing formation we had adopted. Whatever the ships did, *Ohio*'s bow or stern swung dangerously towards the edges of the minefield.

We were stuck just a few miles from safety. One wrong move and we'd be blown up, not by enemy bombs, but by our own mines.

Chapter 13
Ohio Triumphant

We were very lucky not only that there was no wind blowing but also that the Mediterranean has very little tide. Had it been otherwise, we could have ended up in the minefield. After two anxious hours, several tugs arrived from Valletta. They fussed about, pushing, pulling and hooting, and finally eased the raft of ships around until it was pointing in the right direction. Very slowly, slung between the destroyers, *Ohio* began the last leg of her voyage to Valletta.

As it grew light we were able to get our first real look at Malta. It is a rocky island with few trees and the fierce August sun had burned everything brown. Every vantage point along the coast was lined with people. It seemed as though the whole island had turned out to watch us come in. They knew that what had already arrived would keep them going, but without *Ohio*'s kerosene and fuel oil the evil day of surrender had only been postponed a little.

Most of our convoy's original close escort was now on its way back to Gibraltar, but as we were turned towards the entrance of Grand Harbour we were hailed by Commander Swain.

'I've just received a signal for you from Admiral Burrough,' he shouted. 'It reads: TO MV OHIO STOP I AM PROUD TO HAVE MET YOU MESSAGE ENDS. That goes for us, too, Captain.'

'We're here thanks to you chaps,' called Mason. 'It's not over yet and I don't think she's long left. I just hope it's long enough.'

The sea had already lapped on to the deck when the destroyers cast off, their places being taken by tugs. We approached the harbour mouth, and there were the massive fortifications we had seen so often on the newsreels – Fort St Elmo to starboard and Fort St Angelo to port. Every possible space seemed to be crammed with people. We could hear cheering and the sound of a band. The tugs began to hoot and the warships sounded their sirens. Mr Barton, once more the naval officer, turned smartly to Captain Mason and saluted.

'We're going to be cheered into harbour, sir,' he said. 'She's your ship and it's you they want to see. The usual thing is to stand on top of the bridge.'

I think we were all immensely relieved to have arrived, and proud of what we had achieved, too, but the sight made us feel rather humble as well.

'Will you look at that!' I said. 'Just listen to them!'

I think Bill had a bit of a lump in his throat; I know I did.

'Just think what *they've* been through,' he said. 'And now they've come out to cheer *us!*'

You could live a thousand lives and never experience what we did then. On the damaged breakwater a band was playing 'Rule Britannia'. As we moved up the wreck-strewn harbour, the cheers were deafening. The crowds were jammed solid, waving anything they could get their hands on. There were men, women, children and our own garrison, shouting their heads off.

The Maltese are very religious and some of the older people were in tears. We had brought the *Ohio* in on 15 August, on which they celebrate the Festival of Santa Maria, and they thought it was a miracle; so it was. We cheered back and so did the warships' crews, stripped to the waist and with empty shell cases rolling round their feet. When we passed the battered *Port Chalmers*, *Rochester Castle* and *Melbourne Star*, their crews gave us a terrific cheer, too.

Then, as the tugs were heaving us in towards our berth, we saw Mr Gray, the first officer, Mr Wyld, the chief engineer, and the rest of our crew waiting for us. They had already made arrangements for our arrival, so everything went smoothly. We drew in alongside a sunken tanker, the *Plumleaf*, that had gone down beside the quay, and scores of hands quickly made us fast. Hoses snaked aboard and were soon pulsating as our precious cargo was pumped into safe underground tanks. Another tanker, the *Boxall*, came alongside and began filling her own tanks from ours.

There was more cheering from the harbour entrance. The *Brisbane Star*, which we had given up for lost, was coming in, down by the bows but still under her own steam. There were people swarming all over the *Ohio*. She was no longer our ship and we were no longer needed. It was a strange feeling. Captain Mason came down from the bridge. Now that it was all over he looked terribly tired; he seemed to have aged years since I first saw him at Greenock.

Temporary accommodation had been arranged for us ashore. We left the ship in the care of Mr Gray and his party. I was deadly tired but it was too hot to sleep and I was unable to relax. I walked back to the quay beside the *Ohio* and sat with my legs dangling over the edge, watching them pump out her tanks. I must have been there for a few hours, because she settled lower and lower until it was clear she was finally resting on the harbour's muddy bottom. The pumping stopped and a gang of Maltese workmen came ashore from her. Their foreman, a middle-aged man with brown eyes set in a kindly face, sat down beside me, wiping his hands on an oily rag.

'Oil is lighter than water,' he explained. 'But when we pumped it out sea water took its place in the damaged tanks. That made the ship heavier and finally she has broken her back. She will not sail again. She was your ship?'

'Yes, she was my ship,' I replied.

'You are brave men, all of you,' he said. 'To the Maltese people you are heroes.'

I shrugged. I didn't want to tell him that there had been times out there when I had been scared stiff.

'At home we say that the people of Malta are heroes.'

Now it was his turn to shrug.

'Sometimes it is difficult to be brave,' he said. 'Sometimes, one does not feel like being brave, but everyone round us is behaving bravely so we try a little harder. That is the best sort of bravery. You understand that, I think.'

I nodded. It was true that the British and the Maltese seem to have an instinctive understanding of each other. We talked a while longer, then I stood up to go.

'I am sorry about your ship,' he said.

'She made us a promise,' I replied, 'and now she's kept it. I'm proud of her.'

Chapter 14
Malta

Late that afternoon, in the temporary accommodation occupied by *Ohio*'s crew, we gunners were eating our first meal in Malta. It consisted of sardines and dry bread washed down with tea. I was ravenous and food had never tasted better.

'DEMS gunners?' said a voice.

The speaker, a Royal Artillery bombardier, was standing in the doorway. We stared at each other in disbelief. His clean appearance, shiny boots and pressed khaki drill seemed to belong to another world. We were all filthy, unshaven and our uniforms were torn and stained.

'I've got a truck outside waiting to take you up to the barracks,' he said. 'Once you've settled in, it looks as though you lot will need kitting out.'

At that moment Captain Mason appeared, having come to see us off personally. He shook hands with each of us in turn.

'Thank you for all you've done,' he said. 'They did everything they could think of to stop us, but we didn't let them, did we?'

When Mason had left, I went looking for Bruce Cameron. I found him down by the dock.

'Cheerio then, sir,' I said. 'One of these days you'll be skipper of your own ship – I'll take bets on it.'

He looked at me shrewdly, his crooked grin starting to show.

'I had you down as a cheeky blighter when you came aboard, but there's more to you than that. By the way, I've been meaning to thank you for helping me out back there. Maybe we've both learned something this voyage. You still want to be a field gunner?'

I shook my head.

'No,' I said. 'Out there it didn't matter whether you were Royal Artillery, Royal Navy or Merchant Navy – we all got on with the job and we finished it. That'll do me and I'm happy to stay as I am.'

'Where to now?' he asked.

'I don't know,' I said, shrugging. 'I'll go where they send me. How about you?'

'Well, I reckon I've had all the excitement I want for the moment. When this is over, I'm applying for a nice quiet job – maybe third mate on a Sydney Harbour Ferry!'

'I'll believe that when I see it, sir!' I said, and we both laughed.

As the truck drove away from the dock area we could see the battering Malta had received. Even those buildings which hadn't been flattened had been badly knocked about. They were built from square stone blocks, which lay about everywhere.

'This is the most heavily bombed place on earth,' said the bombardier, reading our thoughts.

'There don't seem to be many people about,' Ron commented.

'No. Some of the Maltese have been evacuated to the island of Gozo and some have moved out into the country. Most of the rest have adapted themselves to living underground in cellars, bunkers and tunnels.'

Looking at the devastation, I could only marvel at the way these courageous people had stuck by us through thick and thin. No wonder the king had awarded the George Cross to the entire island.

We arrived at Fort St Rocco, which provided accommodation for a coastal defence battery and an anti-aircraft unit. It was situated on a hill from which you could see the entrance to Grand Harbour. As the lads were being shown into their billet I saw a sergeant walking down the path between the huts.

'Excuse me, Sarge!' I said. 'Do you happen to know a Sergeant Dick Smith?'

'You'll find him over in the AA gun position,' he replied.

I walked across. The gun crews were relaxing but I spotted Dick at once. There he was, smart in khaki drill, bronzed and much leaner than when I'd last seen him. His back was to me and he was resting one hand on the gun as he stared out to sea. I paused, because his figure seemed to represent everything Malta had come to stand for – courage, endurance and everlasting defiance to the enemy.

Suddenly aware of my presence, he turned and glared at me.

'What are you looking at, soldier?'

'Aye aye, Dick!' I said. 'Aren't you going to say hallo, then?'

Finally recognizing me, Dick looked at me as though he'd seen a ghost.

'John? What are you doing here?'

'I'm just off the *Ohio*.'

'The *Ohio*! We watched you come in – we wondered whether you'd make it.'

We hadn't seen each other for over two years and just stood there shaking hands, slapping each other on the back and laughing like a pair of idiots.

'How are Mam and Dad?' he asked.

'I saw them last month and they're fine. Mam says you don't write often enough.'

'Doesn't she know we've been under siege here?'

'She'd say that's no excuse and you should try harder!'

We were both still roaring with laughter when the sharp voice of authority broke in.

'Sarn't Smith! Who is that scruffy article you're talking to?'

We turned to find a sergeant-major glaring at us. His khaki drill was immaculate, his cane was at the correct angle under his arm, his moustache bristled and his eyes bored into me.

'He's my kid brother John, sir,' said Dick. 'He's just off the *Ohio*.'

It seems even sergeant-majors can be human at times. I watched his fierce expression dissolve into a smile.

'We've been hearing about the terrific scrap you fellows put up,' he said. 'I'll always be glad to shake the hand of a man who served aboard the *Ohio*!'

Yes, I had served aboard the *Ohio*, and many more men would shake my hand because of it. It was an experience I'd never forget and I was very proud to have played my part. I had a feeling somehow that people would remember the *Ohio* too, even though her active 'life' had come to an end in Malta's Grand Harbour.

Pedestal and After

What might have happened to the Pedestal convoy if the Italian surface fleet had intervened, no one can say for certain. Admiral Burrough was aware that Italian ships were at sea and, in view of the small size of his close escort, this must have given him serious anxiety. In the event, the Italian Navy was half-hearted about the involvement of its heavy surface warships and allowed itself to be bluffed by the RAF. On 13 August HM submarine *Unbroken*, commanded by Lieutenant Alastair Mars, torpedoed the heavy cruiser *Bolanzo* and the light cruiser *Attendolo* off the north-east coast of Sicily while they were returning to base; neither played much further part in the war.

Several days after the Pedestal convoy arrived, a report in a neutral Swiss newspaper quoted official Italian sources as saying that, in view of the quantity of supplies delivered to Malta, the island's surrender could no longer be expected .

On Malta itself, Pedestal's supplies enabled the rations to be increased very slightly. Of even greater significance was the fact that submarines and aircraft based on the island immediately resumed their attacks on Axis shipping.

In the mean time, air attacks on Malta continued, though at a reduced level. In October 1942, however, in a last desperate bid to subdue the island, some 600 Axis aircraft mounted a nine-day air offensive. Over 100 bombers were shot down in exchange for only 30 British fighters, many of the latter's pilots being able to parachute to safety. In November, another convoy, code-named Stone Age, successfully fought through to Malta from Alexandria in Egypt. Four more convoys arrived the following month. The worst of the island's ordeal now lay in the past.

The island of Malta was awarded the George Cross in April 1942 and, after the Axis armies had surrendered in Tunisia, King George VI made a personal visit to it and received a tremendous welcome. The crew of the *Ohio* were also recognized.

Captain Dudley Mason was awarded the George Cross, the highest award for gallantry a civilian can ever receive and the equivalent of the Victoria Cross awarded by the military. Captain Mason, exhausted by the effort of bringing his ship through, spent some time in hospital recovering. Among other awards made for the operation was that of the Distinguished Service Medal to Bombardier Labarn, who commanded the Royal Artillery detachment aboard the *Ohio*.

As for *Ohio* herself, she had indeed broken her back but was refloated, patched up and served as a stores and accommodation ship in Grand Harbour for the rest of the war. Repairing her would have cost more than she was worth, so on 19 September 1946 her two halves were towed out to sea to be used as gunnery targets until they finally sank.

What the *Ohio* and her crew achieved lives on in many men's minds. Admiral of the Fleet Sir Philip Vian described her as 'famous, fabulous, never to be forgotten'. Her name-plate and other items connected with the ship have a prominent place in the Malta War Museum, situated in Fort Elmo. In 1959 the Red Ensign which she flew throughout the Pedestal operation was presented to the

Imperial War Museum in London by the Eagle Oil and Shipping Company.

What happened next?

The success of the Pedestal convoy's mission had a significant effect on the Allies' situation in the Mediterranean and on the Desert War being fought in North Africa:

● The success of Pedestal enabled Malta to hold out against the Axis powers until larger convoys brought in further supplies. This ensured Allied domination of the central Mediterranean.

● Submarines and aircraft based in Malta were able to resume attacks on Axis shipping. As a result, during the second Battle of Alamein in Egypt, which commenced on 23 October 1942, the Axis forces never had more than a few days' supply of fuel at any one time, which greatly weakened their position.

● Malta became the springboard for the invasion of Sicily in June 1943, which led directly to the collapse of Italy and its eventual surrender.

Losses During Pedestal
Allied

Warships

***Eagle*, fleet aircraft carrier** torpedoed and sunk by U-73 on 11 August 1942

***Manchester*, cruiser** torpedoed by motor torpedo boats, scuttled on 13 August 1942

***Cairo*, anti-aircraft cruiser** torpedoed and sunk by Italian submarine *Axum* on 12 August 1942

***Foresight*, destroyer** torpedoed during air attack, sunk by HMS *Tartar* on 12 August 1942

***Indomitable*, fleet aircraft carrier** suffered bomb damage on 12 August 1942

***Kenya*, cruiser** torpedoed by Italian submarine *Alagi* on 12 August 1942

***Nigeria*, cruiser** torpedoed by Italian submarine *Axum* on 12 August 1942

***Ithuriel*, destroyer** bows damaged while ramming Italian submarine *Cobalto* on 12 August 1942

Merchant Vessels

Deucalion damaged and sunk by a second air attack on 12 August 1942

Empire Hope sunk during an air attack on 12 August 1942

Clan Ferguson sunk during an air attack
on 13 August 1942
Santa Elisa sunk during a torpedo boat
attack on 13 August 1942
Glenorchy sunk during a torpedo boat
attack on 13 August 1942
Almeria Lykes sunk during a torpedo boat
attack on 13 August 1942
Wairangi sunk during a torpedo boat
attack on 13 August 1942
Waimarama sunk during an air attack on
13 August 1942
Dorset sunk during an air attack on
13 August 1942
Ohio bomb and torpedo damage
Brisbane Star bomb and torpedo damage
Melbourne Star bomb damage
Port Chalmers bomb damage
Rochester Castle bomb and torpedo damage

In addition to the service personnel
killed, 350 officers and men of the
Merchant Navy lost their lives during
Pedestal.

Aircraft

Sixteen aircraft were lost aboard *Eagle*.
Given the dangerous nature of the
operation and the overwhelming strength
of the enemy, the losses suffered by the
RAF and Fleet Air Arm were not as bad as
had been expected, amounting to seven and
thirteen respectively destroyed in
combat.

Axis
Warships

Dagabur, **submarine** sunk
Cobalto, **submarine** sunk
Bolanzo, **heavy cruiser** damaged
Attendolo, **light cruiser** damaged

Several torpedo craft also damaged

Aircraft

The Luftwaffe (German airforce) lost
nineteen aircraft and the Regia
Aeronautica (Italian airforce) lost
forty-two. The number of planes lost by
the Axis powers was only a small part of
their entire force.

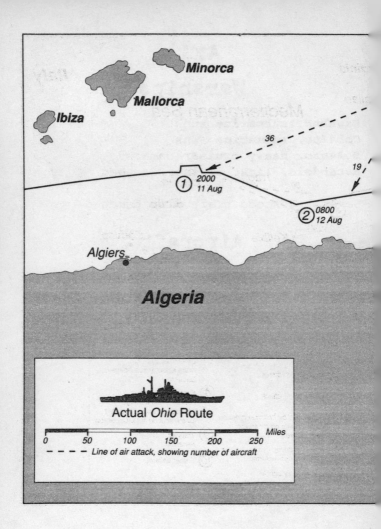

Minorca

Mallorca

Ibiza

36

19

① 2000
11 Aug

② 0800
12 Aug

Algiers

Algeria

Actual *Ohio* Route

0	50	100	150	200	250

Miles

– – – – Line of air attack, showing number of aircraft

Mediterranean Sea

Sardinia

Cagliari

Italy

Trapani •Palermo

Sicily

Comiso

Kelibia

Tunis

Tunisia

Malta Channel

Malta

0800
13 Aug

Noon
13 Aug

① Beats off air attack.

② Beats off air attack.

③ Beats off air attack.

④ Torpedoed by Italian submarine
Axum. Beats off air attack.
Fire aboard.

⑤ Follows convoy
after engines restarted.

⑥ Beats off air attack.
Dive bomber crashes aboard.

⑦ Beats off air attack.
Bomb damage.
Abandoned and re-boarded.
Under tow.

⑧ Beats off air attacks.
Further bomb damage.
Abandoned and re-boarded
for the second time. Under tow.

⑨ Trapped in British
minefield.

⑩ Enters Valletta.

War Rations
Great Britain

Rations for the people of Great Britain
in mid-1942.
(Per person per week.)

Bacon and ham ....4 oz
Sugar.....................................8 oz
Butter....................................2 oz
Cooking fats ....8 oz
Tea.......................................2 oz
Cheese...................................1 oz
Jam.......................................2 oz
Meat (by price) ......1 shilling (5 pence)

In addition to the above, each person was
also allowed sixteen points per month that
they could save up and use to buy luxury
goods when they were available. Bread was
not as good quality as during peacetime
but supplies were adequate. Vegetable
supplies were also adequate. Apples, pears
and plums were available in season, but
tropical fruits were very rare.

People could increase their rations by
catching rabbits or fish. Many people
grew vegetables in their gardens or on an
allotment and keeping hens for eggs was
also popular. Cooking was done by coal
gas or electric cookers or a solid fuel
kitchen range. People had to be very
careful not to use too much domestic
coal.

Malta

Actual rations for the people of Malta, during the time of the Pedestal Convoy. (Per person per week.)

Bread..................................	73 oz
Fats....................................	3 oz
Cheese	1¾ oz
Coffee	1¼ oz
Goat's milk	3 pints
Tomatoes...........................	3 lbs
Potatoes	1½ lbs

There was no sugar, rice, tea, oil, butter, meat or soap available. Supplies of fresh vegetables were not very regular but some fish could still be caught. Each person was allowed eight gallons of water per day for all purposes, including drinking, washing and cooking. During the worst of the siege, the daily diet consisted of soup and bread.

Malta has no natural supplies of wood or coal so kerosene was used for cooking. By the time the Pedestal Convoy set off, the island's stock of kerosene, plus the stocks of wheat and flour, had run out. The coal brought to the island for use by the power station ran out in June and so there was no electricity available in people's homes. Stocks of aviation spirit, fuel oil and ammunition were only expected to last until the middle of August.

Ohio enters Grand Harbour, Malta.

What was it actually like to land and fight in Normandy during the Second World War? Find out in the next *Warpath* book, *Beach Assault*.

'Ah, here's the problem,' said George, indicating two faulty connections.

We fixed them and scrambled back aboard.

'Stand by,' said George.'Firing – now!'

Nothing happened. As we went out again I could see that George was close to despair. He had done everything possible, yet still the Goat refused to fire. We checked connections again and found nothing out of place. I began checking the main lead back to the AVRE, running my fingers along it inch by inch.

At one point I felt a roughness and saw that it had been nicked. When I opened the insulation, several torn strands of copper wire were revealed.

'Got it!' I said. 'It looks as though it's been cut by a bullet.'

'Good lad!' said George approvingly. 'Well, we'll soon have that fixed.'

It only took minutes, although it seemed like hours as he exposed the broken wires, carefully rejoined them and bound them with tape, humming all the time.

'Right!' he said. 'Let's have another go, shall we?'

Once more, we clambered aboard.

'Stand by! Firing – now!'

There was a thunderclap explosion. The huge doors were hurled inwards off their hinges, seemed to hang for a second and then collapsed in a cloud of dust and smoke.

'Nice one, Mr Bang!' said Jock. 'That's one o' ye're best yet!'

When the smoke cleared I could see that the doors were lying on top of the portcullis, one side of which had been torn out of its groove. Half the other side was still in place, leaving the twisted grille at an angle with the doors lying on top. Beyond, I could see figures running in the fort's courtyard and several shots came our way.

'Reckon you can get us over that?' asked Ron.

'Yes, I think so,' I replied. The weight of the

vehicle should bring down the rest of that ironwork.'

'Off you go, then. Mike, Gloomy, give 'em all you've got!'

I let in the clutch, increasing power to the engine. Slowly, the AVRE began climbing the ramp created by the fallen doors. There was a sound of twisting, tearing metal as the portcullis was ripped free of its last restraint. The pile of debris collapsed beneath us but I kept going.

Beside me, Gloomy was hammering away with his machine gun. The confined space of the gateway tunnel magnified the sound many times. As we emerged, we came under heavy fire from several directions. Mike let fly with the petard, bringing down part of a barrack block opposite. Ron shouted a warning.

'Gloomy – Don't reload! You'll get your miserable head blown off!'

We cruised round the courtyard, machine gunning for all we were worth.

'Where's everyone else?' I shouted.

A man with a panzerfaust, the German equivalent of the bazooka, darted out of a doorway ahead of us. He took hasty aim, fired, and disappeared quickly. The bomb exploded against the starboard air intake. It did not penetrate the main armour, but the blast caused the engine to cut out. It took a full minute for me to re-start it and still no other AVRE's arrived.

'Without support we've got no chance,' shouted Gloomy.

In that second, a horrible, icy thought shot through my mind – this is where you're going to die!